STAYING JEWISH

AND

SURVIVING

COLLEGE

SURVIVAL GUIDE
FOR THE
JEWISH STUDENT
AT COLLEGE

By Paul Silverman

ISBN # 0-9673007-0-3
Library of Congress #95-92375

For more information please write to:

 JUDAIC RENEWAL PRESS ✡

P.O. BOX 31095
HOUSTON, TX 77231
(281) 722-3883
or visit our web site at
www.Jewishcollegestudents.com

Printed in the United States by:
Morris Publishing
3212 East Highway 30
Kearney, NE 68847
1-800-650-7888

Staying Jewish and Surviving College is dedicated in memory of my grandmothers

Cecilia Silverman

Dena Horn

SPECIAL THANKS TO:

My mom, who without her help, I would have never been able to go to college and experience everything I wrote about.

Donna, my beautiful wife. Had I not followed everything I wrote about, I never would have retained my Jewish identity and found someone as special as you. I love you very much.

My nieces, Adriel, Ariel and Madeline, and my nephews, Daniel and Joshua, you are my life.

Kenny, my best friend, thanks for always being there and encouraging me to reach my goals.

Paul, my best friend in North America.
Thanks for always being there the last few years and especially the "Summer of 21".

The Brothers of Delta Tau Delta, without your constant reminders of my faith, I might have forgotten I was Jewish. Thanks for helping me remember.

TABLE OF CONTENTS

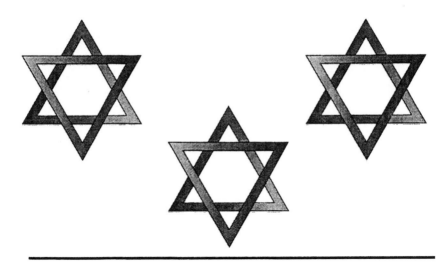

INTRODUCTION

Throughout college life, I was faced with many challenges to my Judaism. As I reached out for answers, I found that they were few and far between. As I went to local bookstores to find answers, I found many books dealing with Judaism, yet none on how to religiously adjust to the college environment. I also found very little, or nothing, on how to adjust to the general aspects of being away at college. It was then that I decided something needed to be done. That is when I decided to write this book.

The purpose of this book is to guide you and give you suggestions on how to deal with various aspects of Jewish living in the college environment. In addition, it can also help you adjust to the more secular aspects of college life that are not usually associated with religious life. It is not meant to preach to you or impose religious or moral lessons.

The book is divided into four parts:

1. Jewish survival
2. General college survival
3. Prayers for special occasions
4. Appendix of Jewish resources

The content of the chapters is an accumulation of what many others and I experienced in college. You won't necessarily experience all of them, as you might also experience some things that aren't covered in the contents of this book.

In writing this book, I tried to take a realistic and moderate approach to my suggestions and advice. I realize that if I were to tell you to go to Synagogue every Friday night and never drink, you probably wouldn't read this book much less take the advice that's in it. Therefore, I will only give you suggestions and real life experiences to help you make the decisions that will affect your life at college.

To give you an idea of my qualifications for writing this book, I will tell you a bit about myself and my college life.

I was raised at a conservative congregation in Houston. I went to a Jewish day school from the time I was in diapers until sixth grade. After that, I was put into the public school system, and my parents switched to a reform congregation. Before graduating from high school, like you, I had to decide which college I wanted to attend. For various reasons, I chose Stephen F. Austin State University in Nacogdoches, Texas. Nacogdoches has a population of 35,000, and is located in East Texas, about three hours north of Houston. In this part of the state, *Jewish* is close to an unknown word, and the closest synagogue is an hour and a half away. Most of the area is Southern Baptist or Pentecostal. With a population of 12,000 students, Nacogdoches has more religious diversity than the rest of East Texas.

When I first got to SFA, I joined the Jewish Student Fellowship. The group wasn't as large as most Hillel chapters, but due to our location and low Jewish population, this was to be expected. After joining the Jewish Student Fellowship, I joined my fraternity Delta Tau Delta.

Throughout my college life, I had to handle many of the problems in the following chapters. Through these experiences, I realized that there were correct and incorrect ways of handling situations that affected me religiously and personally.

I have now graduated, and I hope that I can make a difference in the lives of Jewish college students through passing on the lessons I learned through time, patience, and being Jewish. I hope you find this book useful, and it makes you comfortable in your new environment at college. In addition, I hope that it helps lead you on the path to a wonderful Jewish life. So sit back, read, laugh, and learn.

SECTION
1
JEWISH
SURVIVAL

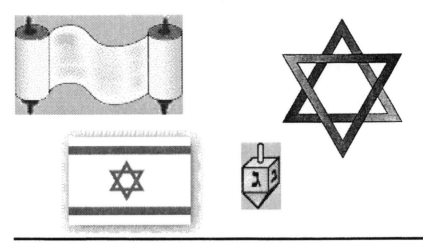

CHAPTER 1

KEEPING YOUR JEWISH IDENTITY

> "Yes, I am a Jew, and when the ancestors of the
> right honorable gentlemen were brutal savages,
> mine were priests in the Temple of Solomon."
>   - Benjamin Disraeli

The most important thing to do while in college and
through life is to keep your Jewish identity. You are a Jew.
You were born one (most likely), you are still one, and you
will die one. Being a Jew means you are part of a strong
religion, culture, and way of life. You should never try to hide
it. Being Jewish is something you should be proud of. For
those of you who have seen the movie "*School Ties*,"
you saw that David Green's worst mistake was taking off

his Star of David. You don't have to go around your dorm singing "Adon Olam" and waving an Israeli flag, but you don't need to hide your faith.

Religious Environment

One thing that greatly affects your religious identity is your religious environment. No matter how many Jewish students are at your school, you will still most likely be a minority. Even though your high school may have been similar, the religious environment at college changes a lot. The religious groups at college are larger, more involved, and greatly expand their efforts to recruit new members. Don't be surprised when they try to recruit you. You have probably heard about, but have never been approached by missionaries. During your college career, at least one will approach you. In addition, even the students that aren't missionaries, but involved in religious groups, will ask questions about Judaism. Although I enjoyed answering these questions, at first it took me by surprise.

Promoting Your Identity to Others

Promoting your identity means letting people know that you are Jewish. There are two ways of doing this: actively and passively.

There are many ways to actively promote your identity. The easiest way is to tell someone that you are Jewish. This is very simple and to the point. I wouldn't suggest renting a billboard and advertising, but when someone asks tell them the truth. Most of the time, the person will say something positive, and that's the end. If an anti-Semitic slur is said, don't worry, we'll get to that in a later chapter. Another way you can tell people you are Jewish is by everyday conversation. When someone asks if you went to Church for Easter, that's a good time to tell them you are Jewish.

The passive ways to promote your Jewish identity range from symbols such as the huge Israeli flag I had in my dorm room to displaying the small Torah you probably received when you were consecrated. The purpose of this is to announce your faith. When people walked into my room and saw my Israeli flag, they instantly knew I was Jewish.

Sometimes you can combine the physical and verbal ways. Very few people that saw the Mezuzah on my door knew what it was much less what it signified. Not only did it promote my identity, but it was a great time to tell them I was Jewish when they asked what it was.

I would strongly recommend that you display something that shows you are Jewish . Not only does it promote your faith to others, but it also reinforces your own personal religious identity.

Promoting Personal Identity

Of all the people you promote your faith to, promoting Jewish identity to yourself is by far the most important.

Unless you live at home while in college, you won't have the same reminders of your faith or community. The Temple you use to drive by and think about your Bar/Bat Mitzvah is miles away. The Jewish Community Center you went to camp at is miles away. Your home with all the Jewish art, culture, and meaning is also far away. All of these factors that reinforce your religious identity you will not see again until you go home. You will be surprised how much meaning these religious places have to you when they are no longer observable.

As you can now see, there is a lot that goes into your

external Jewish identity. By now you're probably thinking that your personal Jewish identity is doomed, and there is nothing you can do. Remember, in the introduction I told you that the purpose of this book is to help you not scare you, so here are some ways to retain your Jewish identity.

Physical Objects and Symbols

Earlier in the chapter, I told you about how physical objects and symbols can reinforce your external identity. Now, let's talk a bit more about how they reinforce your internal Jewish identity.

Because our faith has such a long history and holds such a strong meaning, we have many symbols with many meanings. There are three basic types of symbols: symbols of religious meaning, symbols of personal meaning, and symbols of culture.

The first type, religious meaning, is obvious. These have high religious symbolism and meaning to all Jews. Some examples include: Stars-of-David, Mezuzahs, Siddurs, Torahs, Tallit, etc. The purpose of these symbols is to remind you of the theological aspects of Judaism. No matter how many Christmas trees are around you, these symbols will remind you of the core of Judaism.

The second type, personal meaning, only has significance to you or your family. Items on this list would include a program, picture, or a video from your Bar/Bat Mitzvah, pictures of your trip to Israel, or anything else you can reminisce about. These will be there to remind you of specific Jewish related events. Another item on this list is a scrapbook from any youth related activities such as USY, TEFTY, or AZA /BBG's. This will help you remember all your Jewish friends, and the wonderful time you had with them.

The third type, cultural symbols, relates to our culture rather than pure religion. These include books, movies and anything else that relates to culture more than theology. The purpose of these is to remind you of our culture.

Even though I have separated these into three distinct categories, some of them can be combined. For example, "Fiddler on the Roof" is a very good symbolic reminder of our religion and our culture.

As I stated before, I think it is vitally important to take one or more of these symbols with you to college. These will take the place of other symbols and places that won't be there to remind you of your religion. They will constantly remind you that no matter where you are or what the religious culture of your school is, your Judaism is still there. Because these symbols have reinforced our identity for over 5,000 years, I'm sure they will be around for at least four more years while you are in college. If you are on the "extended plan" like I was, make that six more years.

Religious Observance

The next area of keeping your personal religious identity has to do with something more than just symbols; it has to do with religious observance. Religious observance refers to how often you go to Synagogue, the Jewish laws and customs you keep, and any other activities that bind you to your faith and culture.

You will probably find that this area changes drastically when you leave the religious environment in which you were raised. Here is an example of what might happen and some suggestions on how to deal with the situation.

Most of the time when you go to Synagogue while living at home, your parents take you. Unfortunately, how often do you take your parents? In addition, the laws and customs that you follow are largely the result of your parents. What will you do at college without them there to guide you? Will you fast on Yom Kippur if they are not there to tell you to? These things help build your identity, and without your usual guidance, how will your Jewish identity survive?

Obviously, the best way to deal with these questions is to be involved in Hillel or other Jewish clubs. These clubs vary from school to school. Some might have large groups that have their own buildings. Then again, some might only have five or six members. Regardless of their size, get involved in them. Remember, not only do physical and personal symbols reinforce your Judaism, but so do people. What better way to keep your Jewish identity than being around Jews!

Another way to keep your identity is to find a Temple or Synagogue where you feel comfortable. Again, how often you go is up to you.

Building Your New Identity

The next area of Jewish identity isn't about hiding your identity; it deals with building your new one. As I stated before, when you are away from your parents, your usual religious structure is gone. This is a vital period in your religious life for many reasons.

The main reason is that at this time you are maturing to the point where most of the controls of your life are put in your hands. During this period, you begin to make your own decisions and live life for yourself with your own rules. Religion is one of these decisions you make. You make the decision whether or not you will go to Temple. You make the decision whether or not to fast on Yom Kippur. You make the decision whether or not to date non-Jews. Like all your other new found rights, don't abuse these either. Even though you are now in control of your religious destiny, don't make the choices convenient, make them meaningful. You might find it convenient to not go home for the High Holidays, but you know how empty you would feel by making this choice. Remember, Judaism is a great religion, but you are going to have to make some sacrifices. So far, I have yet to find any of these sacrifices too hard to make.

Science vs. Religion

The next part of identity building has to do with what you learn in your classes. While I enjoy science immensely, it is the one biggest destroyers of faith. Please realize that religion and science both have evidence to prove their perspective. The choice then becomes whether you want to live your life based on strong culture, family, faith, and happiness or on formulas and theories that are disproven every few years. Personally, I'll take Adam and Eve over the Big Bang Theory any day of the week.

I will say, however, that it is possible to combine the two. I do believe in some forms of gradual evolution of animals and planets, but not in the way science does. The problem is, again, no matter how much "proof" is found, very few scientific theories are able to be proven. Remember, evolution means a change in many aspects and doesn't try to just prove that we came from monkeys. Also, evolution doesn't try to prove that God didn't create the heavens and the earth, it just disagrees with religion's version and time table. Evolutionist theories explain how the life that was created has changed, not how it got here in the first place.

Even Charles Darwin, the father of evolution, in his book *The Origin of Species* wrote, "There is a grandeur in this way of life, with its several powers, having been originally breathed by the Creator into new forms or into one..." Therefore, not only religion but evolution also validates the belief in God.

Now, your choice is not between Judaism and science, but between Judaism and atheism. Remember, keeping your identity also means keeping your belief in God.

Conclusion

To sum up, when you go off to college, build your new religious identity. Build from your foundation that you have lived by all your life, don't destroy it. College is a time of learning and enlightenment. This is the best time to build and place Judaism where it belongs: in your heart.

CHAPTER 2

PICKING YOUR DATES AND YOUR FRIENDS

"So long as we are loved by others I should say that we are almost indispensable, and no man is useless while he has a friend."
- Robert Louis Stevenson

One of the most important choices you make that can affect Jewish identity in college is picking your dates and your friends. In the college environment, you will find every type of person from the hard core right wing religious fundamentalist to the militant liberal. Who you choose to associate with can have a big impact on your religious identity.

Before we take a closer look at these two areas, please realize that this book was written to strengthen your Jewish identity and promote Jewish ideals. While some people may get different ideas regarding the message of this chapter, the leading concept is not that we need to be separatists and not associate with other religions and cultures. As I've already stated, other cultures and religions can be a pleasure to learn about.

PICKING YOUR DATES

In keeping with the purpose of this book, I will suggest that you not inter-date. While there might be a very small population of Jewish students at your school, you should try every resource there is to date within the faith. While many people see no harm in inter-dating because it is "just dating, nothing serious," it can turn into something serious very quickly. All inter-marriages have one thing in common – a first date!

Top Five Real Reasons to Date Only Jews
1. Because you know it is the right thing to do.
2. To have the ability to fully express your religious beliefs with someone that fully understands them.
3. To take a step to ensure a Jewish life.
4. To fulfill your duty as a Jew by not compromising your religious identity.
5. To become another link in the 5000 year old chain of our faith.

Top Five Not So Real Reasons to Date Only Jews
1. To be with someone who truly appreciates the taste of gefilte fish.
2. No confusion over the pronunciation of holidays.
3. Complete confidence that you are making your parents happy.

4. To be with someone that will consider Manischewitz wine a fine Merlot.
5. To be with someone whose stomach will growl like a ferocious lion at 6:00 PM on Yom Kippur.

All kidding aside, you know what a meaningful and fulfilling relationship will come out of dating another Jew. When you share your heart with another Jew, you share the same religious beliefs, you appreciate Judaism as a member of the faith, and most importantly, you have the pride and religious fulfillment that you deserve.

Ways to meet other Jews:

1. Get involved in Jewish organizations at school.
2. Attend a local synagogue.
3. Use Jewish internet resources.
4. Agree to go on blind dates. There is a good chance it might work out.
5. Volunteer for Jewish organizations. Many of the administrators and volunteers will have their radar out for eligible people for their sons, daughters, cousins, friends, etc.

PROBLEMS WITH INTER-DATING

There are two main problems with inter-dating: weakening of Jewish identity and inter-marriage.

The first problem with inter-dating is the compromising of Jewish identity. When in love, your heart can overpower rational thought. There are occasions where you are so intent on pleasing the one you are in love with that you will compromise many things that are important to you. A good example of this is as follows: You meet a non-Jewish girl at school who you fall madly in love with. This upcoming weekend is the first night of Passover. Coincidentally, it is also Easter. This new love of yours invites you to come home with her to meet her parents. In trying to please your girlfriend who you are madly in love with, you decide that you will go home to meet her parents. A decision like this occurs quite frequently when a person in love attempts to balance Judaism with inter-dating.

Inter-marriage

Before we start talking about inter-marriage, please realize as it was stated before, this book is to be used to promote Jewish ideas and beliefs. Therefore, I will agree with all three movements of Judaism that have publicly discouraged inter-marriage. While some may be more accepting to inter-married couples, they all have taken the stance to reject the idea itself. The reason for this lies in religious preservation and observance. There has never been a society that has been able to preserve its culture and beliefs when the members themselves don't remain observant.

With the number of inter-marriages rising above 50%, this can only mean a significant reduction in the Jewish population. In addition, only 28% of children from inter-marriages are raised as Jews. While there are quite a few people who have inter-married and maintained their religious identity, many do not. For some, inter-marriage often means the transition from Jewish life into a completely secular life. I assure you that the only way to not be tempted to inter-marry is to not put yourself in an environment that can produce it.

Problems with Inter-marriage

Within all inter-marriages, there is a balance that is attempted between each other's customs and religious practices. While you may agree to allow each other's religious symbols in the house, how comfortable will you be lighting your Menorah that sits next to a nativity scene? Asking someone to compromise their religious beliefs is not fair for either person.

The next reason why you should avoid inter-marriage is the complications in raising children. Whether or not you agree to raise your children Jewish is of not much relevance. If for some reason the marriage doesn't work out, all agreements are void. This happened to someone I know. They agreed to raise their daughter Jewish and have a Jewish home. After the couple's second anniversary, they filed for divorce. Within a year of their separation, the daughter was telling her Jewish father about her religious school classes at church.

Another option for some inter-married couples is to expose the children to both religions and let them choose. While opening Hanukkah and Christmas presents might not confuse the child, explaining the Trinity and then explaining why Jews only believe in one God surely will. Children need guidance and education about religion. Having them choose between Santa Claus and the Macabees is not fair.

Good Points to Marrying Jewish

When I was in college, if I could have known the joys associated with marrying a Jew, I would have never even given a thought to inter-dating much less inter-marriage. A Jewish wedding is not only a religious ceremony, but also a celebration of the continuation of our faith. In addition, it means the beginning of a lifelong relationship based on the happiness of the Jewish religion. I honestly hope that every one of you find out what it's like to be lifted up on a chair during the Hora while all of the most important people in your life cheer you on. The feeling is indescribable.

Another positive to marrying Jewish is the quality of the relationship. Compared to the general population, Jews have lower rates of divorce, infidelity, abuse, and other negative relationship factors. This is not meant to say that non- Jews are bad people, nor is it meant to say that Jews don't experience these negative aspects of relationships. The only thing that is a fact is that these things happen a lot less in Jewish marriages.

Picking Your Friends

Picking your friends is very important. Try not to befriend the first people you come in contact with. Find out through general conversations what people are like before you choose to go out with them.

The best thing you can do to choose friends is to seek those with similar qualities as yourself. Stay away from the wild and crazy people that have no appreciation for life. Many times you will be invited to do things from slam-dancing to drug taking. Again, if you're not a troublemaker, stay away from troublemakers. If you're not sleazy, don't run with sleazy people. Again, as they say, "Birds of a feather flock together." Remember, you are at college to grow intellectually and mentally. Don't revert back to childhood just because you have the freedom. Trying new things and expanding your mind is healthy and expected, but as a teacher of mine said, "Know the difference between fun and stupidity."

The next area of picking your friends has to do with identity and influence. The people at college who are usually looked up to aren't always the best influence. Usually, the guys that pick-up the most girls and the prettiest girls are the ones that are idolized. Don't change your identity to be someone that you're not. Get to know people for themselves and see through the fog that their image portrays. I knew of many people at college who were highly respected for the most trivial reasons, but deep down inside, they were the most uncaring and insensitive people.

The best suggestion I have is to get involved in Jewish groups and meet a "core" of Jewish friends. You will want to have a group of friends that you can go to synagogue and other Jewish events with. In addition, get involved in as many clubs as possible that match your interests.

Conclusion

As I stated before, your identity has a lot to do with the people you choose to associate with. Do your best to find as many quality people who will give you true friendships that you deserve.

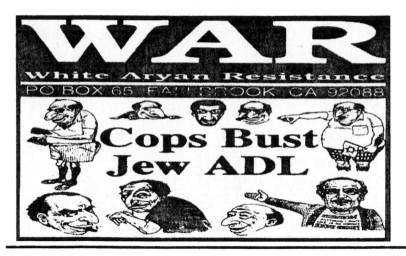

CHAPTER 3

JOKES, RUDE COMMENTS, AND ANTI-SEMITISM

" Never try to reason the prejudice out of a man. It
was not reasoned into him, and cannot be reasoned
out."
- Sydney Smith

" The mind of a bigot is like the pupil of the eye;
the more light you pore upon it, the more it will
contract."
- Oliver Wendell Holmes, Jr.

As you already know, not everyone likes Jews. We
have experienced this throughout history from being slaves
in Egypt to the preachings of Louis Farrakhan today. In the
college environment, there isn't much difference. The hardest job you will have is to separate hatred from humor. You
will learn that there is a difference between the two.

Therefore, we will discuss what to do about jokes, rude comments, and anti-Semitism. Please keep in mind that you might know the difference between the three of these, but people of other religions probably won't. Sometimes a little correcting will be necessary.

I realize that everyone acts differently when it comes to these jokes. There are some Jews that let themselves be trampled on by letting people tell them that all Jews are greedy and cheap and not utter a word in defense. There are also some Jews that laugh at Holocaust jokes with their Christian friends. To me, both of these extremes are wrong.

Now, let's distinguish between the three types of remarks: jokes, rude comments, and anti-Semitism.

Jokes

To begin the discussion about jokes, I will make one generalization for all Jews: don't ever consider anything dealing with the Holocaust a joke. I make this very clear to all of my friends, and you should too.

Now, we will address the acceptable type of jokes, the harmless ones. These are usually said with no hatred toward Jews intended. You know exactly what kind these are. A good example is my fraternity's nickname party. During this party, we would pick out nicknames for each other that were funny and related to the person's character or life. At this party, the two possible nicknames the chapter was going to give me were "Bagel" or "Rabbi." I got to choose which one I wanted, so I was then known by the name "Bagel." While everyone laughed at first, no one meant a single ounce of harm. If anything, it did more good than harm in two ways. First, when I was called "Bagel," it reinforced my Jewish identity. Second, by letting people call me "Bagel," it helped break down the wall between our religions. My fraternity brothers seemed to feel more comfortable in asking me questions about Judaism knowing that I didn't take everything offensively.

In this day of militant political correctness, don't just jump down someone's throat because they laughed at something that relates to your faith. Don't immediately label them an anti-Semite. After all, I'm sure you have made your share of racial jokes, and you're not a racist. If someone says something jokingly, and it offends you, politely let them know how you feel.

Rude Comments

The next area, rude comments, is very common. These include remarks like, "The Jews control the country" and "All Jews are cheap." These comments differ from jokes, because they are clearly meant to harm and discriminate. While many would consider this anti-Semitism, I separate the two. People that make rude comments are usually not anti-Semites or racists. Most of the time they are just stereotyping what family members and society has taught them. There are many ways of handling these comments.

The first way is with what I call "truth confrontation." In doing this, you ask them to validate their remark. If they tell you that Jews are running the country, ask them how. Most of the time, they will just give you a flustered look and dodge the question. If they manage to come up with an answer, most likely it will be so inaccurate it will show. By using "truth confrontation," not only do you defend our religion, you also let the person know that their comments aren't appreciated. The next way to deal with rude comments is with what I call "personal reminders." In doing this, you remind the person of their similar faults. A good example of this happened when one of my college roommates made the comment that Jews are cheap. Instead of using"truth confrontation," I simply reminded him of how excited he got when he found his macaroni and cheese for ten cents cheaper at a warehouse store. After that, I reminded him of his habit of doing his laundry at the dorms where it is free instead of at our apartments. To conclude, I told him that if Jews are so cheap, he would make a great one. That was the last time he brought up "Jewish Economics."

Unfortunately, there are some people who won't respond to either of these two ways. Some of them will insist on making rude comments at every possible chance. These are what I call "borderline anti-Semites." The only way to deal with these people is avoidance. Ignore them, and don't respond in any way to their comments. If they haven't gotten the message by "truth confrontation" or "personal reminders," chances are they are making these comments to irritate you. Don't give them the satisfaction of your time or attention.

As I have stated before, you will be the one to decide the difference between rude comments and jokes. The two golden rules to remember are the source of the comment and the intent.

Anti-Semitism

The last section, anti-Semitism, is by far the most serious. Anti-Semitism is blatant and malicious slander and defamation. With anti-Semitism, you don't consider the intent or the source because it is clearly hatred. Anti-Semitism comes in many evil ways such as violence, aggression, slander, defamation, and mass appeal. Please realize that there is sometimes a fine line between rude comments and anti-Semitism. If a person in your dorm tells you Jews are stingy, that is a rude comment. If your political science professor says it in the middle of class, that is anti-Semitism. Just like you making racial jokes to close friends doesn't necessarily make you a racist, but publishing them in a newspaper does.

Since anti-Semitism is such a serious matter, I will only make two suggestions. First and foremost, call your local Anti Defamation League (ADL) office. They devote their lives to the fight against anti-Semitism and are always more than happy to assist you in any way possible. Even if you aren't sure whether or not an incident is a case of anti-Semitism, call them, and they will tell you. The ADL is an amazing organization and deserves the utmost respect from every Jew.

My second suggestion is to avoid violence. Violence never gets you anywhere except deeper into trouble. The ADL can do a lot more with letters, phone calls, and in a courtroom than you could ever do with a gun, bat, or a book of matches.

Conclusion

Remember that every good thing in life has its price. Your job as a Jew, is to separate, defend, or do what-ever is necessary to deal with jokes, rude comments, and anti-Semitism.

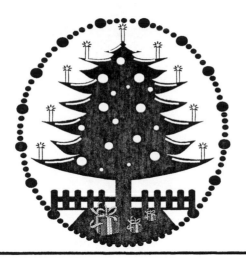

CHAPTER 4

WHY DON'T YOU HAVE A CHRISTMAS TREE?

"More trouble is caused in this world by indiscreet answers than indiscreet questions."
- Sydney J. Harris

By far, this is the question I was asked the most at college. There are many ways to respond to this question. Again, realize that many people know very little or nothing about Judaism. It is not their fault; it's our society's fault. Therefore, you might be their only chance to be educated about Judaism. Often, you will be asked questions that seem extremely ridiculous to you, but they aren't to the person asking them. The worst thing you can do is to laugh at them. It probably took them a great deal of courage to ask; reward their courage with a kind and respectful answer. You will often be asked about customs and practices that deal with other religions. There is no need to justify any Jewish belief to these, just tell them that they are thinking of another religious group. I have been asked many times when I'm going to take my trip to Mecca. Before we look at the specific questions that you may be asked, lets go over methods of answering them.

Methods of Answering

The first thing to remember when answering questions is "simplicity." When someone asks what the paper inside a Mezuzah says, don't tell them it says "Shema Yisrael.." Give them a simple answer like, "It is one of our most important and holy prayers that says that there is only one God." To conclude, tell them it is to Jews what the Lord's Prayer is to Christians. The simpler you keep the answers, the easier it is for them to understand. A long and detailed explanation is worthless if the listener can't comprehend what you are explaining.

The next thing to remember in answering questions is what I call "referral." Try to make your answer remind them of something from their religion. My favorite example of this is when someone asks what my Mezuzah is. I tell them that it is a symbol that represents our religion that we put on our door frames, just like the crucifix that Christians hang in their homes. Again, whenever you can relate our customs to one of theirs, it makes it a lot easier for them to understand. Remember, by answering questions, you are making Judaism less foreign to them. The best way to do this is through association.

Now that you know how to answer questions, let's look at the most frequently asked questions and some appropriate ways to answer. The questions can be divided into three categories: general, symbolic, and personal.

General Questions

The questions that we are asked most are the general questions. They tend to deal with Judaism as a whole rather than specific areas.

The first three questions, "Do Jews believe in God?", "Do Jews believe in Jesus?", and "Why don't Jews believe in Jesus?", can all be answered at the same time. Since Christians believe that Jesus is God, it is sometimes hard for them to understand that although we don't believe in Jesus as the son of God, we still believe in God. To answer this, first tell them that our religion is what they call the "Old Testament," the Torah to us. The reason we don't believe in him like they do is because the Ten Commandments tells us, "Thou shall have no other gods before me." Therefore, since Jesus is supposed to be another form of God, we don't believe in him. To most, this answer will suffice.

The fourth question, which I named the chapter after, "Why don't Jews have a Christmas trees?", is also very common. Even if you have already told them that we don't believe in Jesus, they still might ask you about Christmas trees. Don't get mad or flustered. Many non-Jews feel that Christmas is a secular, or American holiday, more than a religious one. Simply tell them that since we don't believe in the divinity Jesus, there is no reason to celebrate Christmas much less have a Christmas tree. If they still don't understand, ask them if they would have a turkey if they didn't celebrate Thanksgiving.

Another question asked, "Is being Jewish a race?" is very complicated to answer. As you know, being Jewish means that you are from a select group of people with strict beliefs, culture, and way of life. Therefore, how can we not be a race? However, to avoid isolation, I would try to tell them that Judaism is more a way of life than a race. To "refer" them to Christianity ask them if they would consider Amish people to be a race. After all, aren't they a select group of people with strict beliefs, culture, and a way of life? The term race has such a negative image nowadays, try to avoid it if possible.

"Are you a Jew or an American?" is another closely related, but different question. Because we are different from the average American, and we are sometimes considered a "religious" race, people have a hard time grouping us in society. Explain to them that being American is a nationality, and like them, you are an American. Furthermore, you are Jewish, and they are Christian. To combine the two, you are an American Jew, and they are an American Christian. Most likely, they will see the similarity.

The question, "Are all Jews from Israel?" is not asked as much as others. Since Christians are taught that Israel is the Jewish homeland, it's only natural that they associate all Jews as being from Israel. After all, don't we consider all Italians from Italy? To answer this question, give them a brief history lesson. Tell them that even though Israel has always been our religious home, we weren't given the land until 1948. Therefore, our biblical descendants came from there, yet our families came from Europe or wherever your descendants came from. In addition, tell them that Israel is to us what Vatican City is to Catholics.

The next question people might ask is "Why do you have to marry someone who's Jewish?" Assuming that Judaism is important enough to you to marry Jewish, here is an appropriate answer. Tell them that although the Jewish and some non-Jewish ways of life might be similar enough for you to inter-date, they aren't similar enough to marry. Explain that because we believe in the preservation of our religion, inter-marriage is not a Jewish choice. Don't tell them that you wouldn't care, but your parents would. I have heard that statement before, and it makes you look spiritually weak and Jewish parents overbearing.

"What do you do at Temple?" This is another frequently asked question. Since they know very little about Judaism, they know nothing about how we pray. Simply explain to them that like them, we pray to God. We do this in many forms such as in songs, readings, and silent prayers just like they do.

"What are your High Holidays, and why do you celebrate them?" This question is frequently asked around the holidays more than during the year. The most confusing thing for them to understand is Rosh Hashanah because this is when they are exposed to the Jewish Calendar. Most likely, they have never considered that there are other New Years other than that of the Roman Calendar. Explain to them that the Jewish Calendar is our religious calendar. Because of this, our New Year begins on a different day. Tell them that you consider Rosh Hashanah your religious new year, and it is our time for renewal and change just like January 1st for them.

Yom Kippur is very easy to explain. Simply tell them that Yom Kippur is the day we confess our sins and ask for forgiveness. The reason we fast is to repent for our sins. Comparing it to the Catholic ritual of confession usually helps them understand.

"Do Jews think that non-Jews are going to hell?" This is a very hard question to answer because Judaism doesn't concentrate on heaven and hell like Christianity does. Explain this to them and tell them that we don't judge what happens to people of other religions, that's God's job.

"Why do you call yourselves God's chosen people?" To answer this just simply tell them that God chose us to carry on his commandments and teachings, and that is why we are the "chosen people." This is stated in Exodus 19-5, "Now then, if you will obey Me faithfully and keep my covenant, you shall be my treasured possession among all the peoples."

These are most of the general questions that you will be asked. However, be prepared for others.

Symbolic Questions

Symbolic questions are generally about the physical items or specific actions that separate Judaism from Christianity.

The first question under this category is usually, "What are those beanies you wear?" Explain to them they are called Kippot, and they are worn to show respect for God. To refer to Catholics yet one more time, remind them that the Pope wears one too.

"Why do Jews worship that wall in Israel?" This is another frequently asked question. Explain to them that the wall once surrounded one of our holiest Temples and that's why we feel so strongly about it.

"Why do Jews lunge forward and backward when they pray?" Explain to them that it is a part of their religious observance, and it is just a way of enhancing their emotions as they pray just like some Christians holding their hands up when they pray. Also, explain to them that not all Jews practice this, as it is mainly the very observant ones. When explaining this, don't say it in a manner that cheats our more observant members out of the respect they deserve.

The next question, "Why don't some Jews cut their

sideburns?" also deals with our more religious members. To avoid getting into a long explanation of Jewish law, tell them that these people observe every law,whereas you aren't as observant. Furthermore, one of those laws forbids the cutting of the sideburns.

Personal Questions

This area deals with the more personal aspects of Judaism. These are the questions that vary from person to person. Again, to avoid imposing my personal religious views when giving you the answers to these questions, I will merely give you suggestions.

The first thing to remember in answering these types of questions is that if your answers differ from Jewish law, please let them know. If you eat pork, tell them that Jewish law prohibits it, but you eat it anyway. Always remember to give them what Jewish law says about their question first.

The first question, "Do you believe in God?" is very common. The answer to this is different from before because they are asking you for your personal opinion not your religions. When answering this, please give a yes or no answer. Telling them you are not sure or expressing doubt really makes you look confused.

The next question, "What do you think about people of other religions?" is very sensitive in nature. Be as honest as possible when answering this, but always remember to show respect. Personally, I think that Christianity is theologically incorrect, but I would never tell this to one. When I am asked this question, I usually tell them that I don't agree with Christian theology, but I respect everyone's right to freedom of religion. An answer like that is truthful, and very respectful.

Conclusion

While there are many questions that you will be asked about Judaism, these are the questions most commonly asked. Just remember to always answer a question with respect and don't try to impose your theological view.

"Messianic Jews"

"Jews for Jesus"

Cults

CHAPTER 5

NO THANKS, I'M JEWISH

"It is extremely difficult for a Jew to be converted, for how can he bring himself to believe in the divinity of - another Jew."
  - Heinrich Heine

"Religion is a great force - the only real motivivating force in the world; but you must get a man through his own religion, not through yours."
  - George Bernard Shaw

I promise you will use the line, "No thanks, I'm Jewish" at least once. At college, you will be the target of missionaries. There are many ways to deal with them. Some of the missionaries you will respect. Some of them you will learn to accept. Some you will despise. Even if you grow to despise them, they grow to love you because mission-

aries know that Jewish college students are occasionally
lacking a knowledge of the Torah and a sense of spirituality.
They will capitalize on this and try to turn the translations
of the Torah around on you. Don't fall for it! Don't think
that you have to know the Torah from front to back to defend Judaism. Remember, they are trying to convert you;
you don't need any defense.

These groups come in many different forms with
many different styles and tactics.

General Tactics

The main tactic of missionaries is to try to tell you
how passages in the Torah, "Old Testament" to them, refer to
Jesus. I have even been told that Jesus is mentioned in the
Torah. Most likely, you will be told the same thing. Jesus is
never mentioned in the Torah. They try to justify this by
showing you passages that they think refer to Jesus, but
never is his name mentioned.

I admit that there are some passages that could fit
the Christian perspective, but we aren't Christian. Remember, the Torah has produced many different religions based
on different interpretations.

Another one of the missionaries' biggest tactics is to
show you their interpretations of the Torah. Most likely, it is
filled with false interpretations. Don't believe everything
that they show you. As I said before, there are many passages
that they will show you that will fit the story of Christianity
and their leaders. While some of the passages might have
some vague association with a Christian belief, realize that
they describe the story of Jewish history and leaders. I have
studied this at great length and have yet to find one passage
that can't be explained. Remember, they might know more
about the Torah than you do. They can show you a number

of passages that match Christian beliefs. Don't fall for it! Their job is to make you believe in their faith and not doubt your own.

It doesn't matter how much proof or loose associations they come up with, always keep in mind the Second Commandment: "Thou shall have no other gods before Me. Thou shall not make unto thee a graven image, nor any manner of likeness, of anything that is in the heaven above.. Thou shall not bow down unto them, nor serve them..." Exodus 20:3-6. There is no greater defense to Judaism than this. It is very clear that the God that created the heavens and the earth is one. If that doesn't convince you, how about "Hear O Israel, the Lord is Our God, the Lord is One" Deuteronomy 6:25? Needless to say, you have clear proof of your beliefs, they don't.

Before we look at the missionary tactics in depth, remember that no matter what it says in the New Testament, it doesn't matter because according to Judaism, it has no relevance. Obviously, since we don't believe in Jesus, we don't believe in the New Testament. The Koran says a lot about faith, but do Christians believe it? A book is only valid as a testament of faith by those who believe in it.

To begin our study of missionaries, let's look at the different types, their individual tactics, and refuting their claims.

Passive Missionaries

The first type, I call passive missionaries. These are usually Catholics or non-fundamental Protestants. These missionaries are respectful and passive, and they don't fit the usual characteristics of missionaries that are described in the introduction to this chapter. They generally don't believe that they were put on this earth to save you. These missionaries will ask you about your faith in a polite manner.

Usually, if they can tell that you are solid in your beliefs, they will back off. These are the missionaries that you should respect. Although they are concerned with recruiting people into their religion, they always respect the right to freedom of religion. In addition, these missionaries usually don't deal in deception. They are usually straight-forward and honest. Personally, I enjoy talking with this type of missionary. They are so peaceful to talk to that you can comfortably discuss and learn from each other's faith.

Persistent Missionaries

The next type of missionaries are the persistent ones. These are usually the hard core Christian fundamentalists. Most of them do consider it their job and calling in life to save and convert you. Most of the time, they won't take no for an answer. Usually they will question you about your faith and then try to make you doubt it. Don't give in to them! I'm sure if you were to turn their tactics around on them, they would doubt their own religion too. If quoting scripture to you doesn't work, they will usually result to telling you that you're going to hell. This happened to a friend of mine. Instead of getting defensive, he simply told the missionary that he would see him there. Needless to say, the missionary left him alone.

Another tactic they use is to try to capitalize on your emotions. How many times have you heard church slogans like, "We're here for you," "Because he loves you," or one we have in Houston, "The Oasis of Love?" The goal of missionaries is to try to convince you that someone is always there to love you. During a time of extreme mental anguish, like during a break up in a relationship or death of a family member or friend, this might sound very appealing.

You must realize that nothing can heal a broken or lonely heart other than time. While God can help you through these times, He can't fill another person's shoes. Don't ever fall for this form of religious psychotherapy.

To conclude, these types of missionaries should be ignored. Their tactics and beliefs can be so offensive that staying around for their preaching wastes your time. Simply tell them that you are Jewish and walk away. Don't engage in any lengthy conversation with them. After all, if you are happy with your religion, what can these people offer? Not one single thing!

Offbeat Religions and Cults

The next types of missionaries are that of offbeat religions and cults. Whenever approached by these, don't try to justify anything. Don't even tell them what religion you are. These religions and cults often cater to those people that are extremely depressed or isolated and hide it in strange unknown customs. Once they start giving you the love and attention you want, the religious brainwashing begins. Stay as far away from these people as possible! They don't want to just change your religion, they want to change your entire life. In addition, they usually try to take everything you own.

"Jews" for Jesus?

By far, the most deceptive of these missionaries are the so-called "Jews" for Jesus or "Messianic" Jews. This group is the best at turning around the truth and capitalizing on deception. They try to exploit our faith, history, and culture for their twisted purposes. They intentionally target real Jews for conversion. In my hometown of Houston, they set up banners and pass out literature directly accross from the Jewish Community Center. To me, there are few tactics that are more offensive than this.

The main tactic they use is to try to identify with you by telling you that they too are Jewish. However, if they were Jewish, they wouldn't believe in Jesus. They will try to invite you to "temple" with them or any other seemingly normal Jewish event. It will seem to be a normal event at first,then comes Jesus, and slam! Their deception has been revealed.

The next way they try to "save" you is to tell you that Jesus was Jewish. So what? If Jesus was really Jewish, he wouldn't have proclaimed himself to be the son of God. He might have been born Jewish and lived a Jewish life, but that was all voided when he became the basis of Christianity. If you are Jewish, but start your own religion in opposition to Judaism, would your previous faith matter? No. It would be of no relevance. That is precisely what new religions are all about, leaving your old faith and adopting a new one.

These missionaries should be treated like the ones from cults: avoidance. They are not only a disgrace to Jews, but a disgrace to the people that are foolish enough to fall for their deception.

Conclusion

Try to separate the missionaries from the regular religious students. Often a student involved in a religious group or church might invite you to an event out of pure kindness with no religious intent. I was once asked by a student to join him at the Catholic Student Center to hear a guest speaker on a purely secular subject. We went and heard the speaker, and it was quite interesting. Never once did he preach or try to convert me. Another time, the Jewish Student Fellowship rented out the Catholic Student Center for our Jewish Food Festival. To our pleasure, quite a few of the Catholic students attended. We all sat around, talked, ate, and shared our questions and faiths with one another.

The two things to remember when attending other religions events are the type of event and the activity that will take place. Just because you attend other religion's activity, it doesn't mean you are a bad Jew. To fully understand the world we live in, it is a good idea to learn as much as possible about the religions that inhabit it.

To study about missionaries more in depth, read *You Take Jesus, I'll take God* by Samuel Levine. Mr. Levine's fascinating book goes into all of the passages and tactics thoroughly. Ordering information is in the appendix and on our website.

SECTION

2

GENERAL

COLLEGE

SURVIVAL

CHAPTER 6

ENVIRONMENTAL CHANGES

"Change is not made without inconvenience,
even worse to better."
- Richard Hooker

The first thing that will change at college is your environment. It will change not only religiously, but logistically, financially, and socially. How well you adapt to these changes is the key to enjoying college.

Living Environment

Your living environment will be the first to change. You are going from your parents home and under their control to being independent and free. Like me, I'm sure just the thought of this makes you jump with joy. Remember, your mom is not there to tell you to clean up your room anymore, but she also isn't there to cook your dinner or do your laundry. You will find that your new independence has its advantages and disadvantages. During this transition, you will realize how much your parents really do for you.

Roommates

A major way your living environment will change is that you will now have a roommate. This can be a difficult change to get use to.

The first step that should be taken to ensure your transition is to talk to your new roommate before you move in. This gives you a chance to break the ice before the chaos of moving-in takes place. In addition, by talking to them, you can find out who is bringing what so you don't end up with two of everything.

The best way to survive this change is to effectively lay down the ground rules within the first few days. Sit down and have a long talk and discuss what each of you will and won't put up with. Discuss such things as volume of music, overnight guests (shackers), cleaning up, etc. Afterwards, if any complications arise, try to effectively communicate with them, don't argue. Most of the time, an effective conversation can solve any problem. Unfortunately, sometimes you might be stuck with someone who is so selfish and disrespectful that they are impossible to get along with. If this happens, I have one suggestion - move out!

The most important thing to remember about roommates is, like family, there will sometimes be complications. No matter how well you get along with your new roommate, there will be some disagreements.

Campus Safety

The next area of your living environment that you will have to get use to is campus safety. This greatly varies depending on where you are from and where you go to school. Someone from the heart of a rough inner city, that goes to school in rural Vermont, probably knows everything they need to know about crime prevention.

Because all campuses are different, I will make a few general suggestions for safety:

1. Don't ever walk anywhere at night by yourself. Criminals hate groups of people. In addition, find out what parts of your campus are poorly lit at night. Even while walking in groups, stay away from dark areas.

2. Always keep cars doors and dorm rooms locked. Remember, next to date rape, theft is one of the big gest crimes on college campuses.

3. Take self defense classes if they are offered. Not only will these help you in college, but they will help you the rest of your life.

Peer Environment

Another way your living environment will change is through your peers. You will begin to leave that close nit group of high school friends and meet new ones. These new friends will come as a result of school clubs, classes, dorms, fraternities/sororities, etc. They will come from a variety of cultural, economic, and religious backgrounds. This will also be a drastic change. When you are around your Jewish friends, you rarely have to watch what you say, but now you will. You will have to learn how to get to know people. This might sound strange, but when you spend most of your life with one group of friends, it's hard to get to know a lot of new people in a short time. I think it is good to be around a large variety of people, but it takes time to get used to it. Watch out and get to know people before you go out with them. As they say, "Birds of a feather flock together." Make sure you are flocking with the right people.

Financial Environment

The next way your environment will change is financially. No matter how much your parents support you financially, all your new found freedoms will have their price. You will find that in all college towns, there are more ways to spend your disposable income than at home. The businesses in college towns are more focused on entertainment, therefore, attracting you more. The urge to go out all of the time can be very expensive.

Hopefully, you will be advancing socially and going out on more dates than you're use to. This can be very costly because with all of the spare time you now have mixed with the abundance of potential dates, the temptation to go out all the time can become overwhelming.

Watch out for credit cards. Credit card promotions are everywhere on college campuses. The companies know that you are in need of extra funds to satisfy all of your new found freedoms. Stay away from them! Credit cards are almost as addicting as drugs. Before you know it, you can be thousands of dollars in debt. If you apply for a credit card, keep a low credit line and make your payments. Always remember that credit cards are a loan, not a gift.

There are two ways to successfully manage your finances while in college. The first way is to work out a budget. Figure out exactly how much you can spend on partying, food, dates, etc. By knowing your limits, you don't have to worry about getting in any financial binds.

The second way to manage finances also has a lot to do with budgeting; that is when your budget fails, call home. Your parents know that it is difficult to financially adjust to the college environment.

Conclusion

As you have seen, your environment will change in many ways. The key to succeeding in your new environment is time, patience, and a little bit of fun.

CHAPTER 7

EDUCATIONAL SURVIVAL

"The ultimate goal of the educational system is to shift to the individual burden of pursuing his education."

- John W. Gardner

Attendance, studying, papers, and picking your classes are by far the biggest hassles in college. Like many problems in life, there are many ways to deal with these too. Here are some helpful suggestions.

Going to Class

Unlike high school, you won't be put in detention for skipping class. When your alarm goes off, you can hit snooze and sleep until noon. Don't fall into this habit because it becomes addicting. I realize that somedays you will have to miss class due to holidays, sickness, or hangovers, but don't do it excessively. Skipping class excessively can have tons of negative results. Here are a few.

First of all, even though you are in college, some instructors still might take attendance. Most likely, they will deduct from your final grade for excessive absences. If your instructor doesn't take attendance, and the class is small enough, they will notice your excessive absences. At the end of the semester, if you have a borderline grade and need some "extra help," they won't give it to you if you were constantly absent.

The second reason is that even if you have someone take notes, not being there to hear them explained leaves you in the dark. You will have no idea what they mean other than being words on paper.

The third reason not to skip class is because it starts a bad habit of irresponsibility. Realize that when you graduate and get that great job, you won't be used to getting up in the morning. Your professors might tolerate excessive absences, but your bosses won't.

Studying

Yes, I said it, the "S" word. This is by far, the biggest hassle in college. This is an evil fact that interferes with your going out, sleeping late, and watching TV. Unfortunately, it's why you are at college in the first place. Realize that without studying, you will fail. In my years at college, I only met one person who made straight A's and rarely studied. The key thing to remember about studying is not the quantity, but the quality. You will see many people peering at their textbooks until late hours of the morning and still do poorly on their tests. Here are some helpful studying suggestions :

1. Don't cram. Even though your brain is a complex organ, it can't absorb eight chapters in eight hours. Plan ahead and start studying at least a couple of days before your test.

2. Outline your chapters. Usually, at least 25% of all material in textbooks is worthless. Find out what your instructor concentrates on. Some could care less about statistics, dates, or unimportant details. Unless you have an instructor that insists on asking you the unimportant questions on exams, go over the main points.

3. Don't pull all-nighters. Even if you aren't cramming, don't stay up until 4 AM studying. Your brain only works effectively if you are well rested. When you've only had three hours of sleep, you can't even spell your name   much less figure out calculus.

4. Compare your study time to your "party time." If you are partying more than you are effectively studying, you are on a crash course for disaster.

Writing Papers

Writing papers can be either fun or extremely frustrating. Unless you use your resources effectively, you will not find the information you need.

The way to successfully write papers is to get to know your library and its resources . Most librarians will be more than happy to tell you what they offer.

The first step in writing papers is to determine what kind of resources you will need. If you are writing a paper on a current event, first check magazine and journal entries pertaining to your topic. Most libraries have either Infotrack or other systems that will list all of the related articles about your subject that have been written in the last few years. If you are writing on a historical topic, most likely you will want to stick to books.

The second step is to check the internet. With the search engines that are available today, you should be able to find an amazing list of articles on your topic. Don't become an internet addict. If you can't find it on the web, you will be able to find information elsewhere.

The third step to writing papers is to organize your information into specific areas or subjects. This will help you outline your content. Make an outline of main ideas and the order in which they will be written.

The fourth step is to start writing. Don't waste time trying to put the whole paper together in your head. Write it down. With the excessive availability of computers, don't worry about making mistakes and retyping, just start typing. By doing this, you will find that the ideas and sentences will come through your fingers.

The last step is revising and proofreading. Always proofread your paper for mistakes even if you used a spell check. After that, have someone else proofread it. With as many hours as you spend typing and proofreading, I guarantee you will still miss some of your errors.

Picking Your Classes

Next to your friends and your dates, the hardest things to pick are your classes. When you are given your first list of classes at orientation, you will realize what a world of confusion, panic, and chaos registration is. Here is some advice on picking classes.

If you are an early bird, take 8 AM classes. Like me, if you don't get up before noon, take late classes. It doesn't matter how much you want to take a class, if you can't stay awake for it, it's as good as not being there in the first place.

The next step is to list out all of the possible classes you can take and what times they are offered. Next, set up your day, hour by hour, and the possible classes you can take at each time. When the class you need at a certain time is closed, you can then fill in something else from your list of alternatives.

Conclusion

The key to succeeding in college is successfully mastering going to class, studying, and writing papers. If you can succeed at this, you will surely do your best and get the most out of your education.

ΑΕΠ∗ΖΒΤ∗ΑΕΦ∗ΣΔΤ∗ΣΑΜ
ΔΤΔ∗ΑΧΩ∗ΦΔΘ∗ΖΤΑ∗ΘΧ
ΣΑΕ∗ΧΩ∗ΔΧ∗ΠΦ∗ΑΤΩ∗ΔΖ
ΣΧ∗ΔΔΔ∗ΔΣΦ∗ΠΒΦ∗ΤΚΕ
ΓΦΒ∗ΚΣ∗ΣΣΣ∗ΛΧΑ∗ΘΠ

CHAPTER 8

GREEK ORGANIZATIONS

"Fate made us sisters, love makes us friends."
- Author Unknown

Greek organizations have a lot to offer. Looking back on my college years, I can't imagine what I would be like if I hadn't been in one. I learned a lot more important things other than how to drink. Being in a fraternity taught me social and leadership skills, personal responsibility, and much more. In addition, I also made several close lifelong friends.

While your parents might think that you join Greek Organizations to drink and get hazed, most likely they are speaking from inexperience. Don't blame them for this. Most of the time when Greeks are on TV or in the newspaper, it is because some sort of tragedy has happened involving hazing or alcohol. Never once was my fraternity in the newspaper for our project known as Adopt-a-school, where we went and played with underprivileged children.

Never once were we in the newspaper for our Highway Clean-ups. However, when a fight broke out during one of our parties, sure enough, we were on the front page the next day. Now that we have looked at the double standard that Greek Organizations live by, lets look at them in more detail.

Hazing

One of the biggest fears everyone has about fraternities and sororities is hazing. Hazing can be anything from mental interrogation to physical and alcohol abuse. Unfortunately, during the week of rush, nobody will tell you how much you will be hazed. I was once told that there is more acting done by Greeks during the week of rush, than by the theater department the whole year.

One great misconception about hazing is that it only happens in fraternities. This is far from the truth. While most sororities don't haze to anywhere near the extent that fraternities do, some do. The difference is the type of hazing. Fraternities use physical hazing while sororities tend to use more emotional forms.

The national IFC, along with many national fraternities/sororities and schools, have taken measures to end hazing. They include little or no periods of pledgeship. Even though this was a major step to take, it hasn't gotten rid of hazing. All it has done is give chapters less time to haze.

To avoid hazing, I have four suggestions that might help identify when it is happening.First of all, do you have friends in the chapter? If so, they are a good way to find out about potential hazing. While they might not tell you the entire truth, they should give you a pretty good idea. Also, if you know that they wouldn't put up with hazing and they made it through pledgeship, most likely they weren't hazed. Finally, if you know them well enough, you can see if their pledgeship is taking a negative toll on them.

The second way to detect hazing is the physical appearance and condition of the chapter's pledges. When you always see pledges from a certain chapter walking around tired, ragged out, and looking depressed and humiliated, that's probably a good indication that they are being hazed.

The third way to detect hazing is probably the least reliable, but still useful. Even though rumors of hazing fly around campuses about every chapter, there are some that seem to have a well-known reputation of hazing. While there is a slight chance that this reputation is false, don't take your chances. In the three years I was in the Greek system, I heard a lot of false rumors, but I never heard about a known reputation of hazing being false.

The last way to reduce your chance of being hazed is to join a Jewish fraternity/sorority. Although hazing does go on in these, and I know of one who lost their charter for hazing, the aspect of religion greatly bonds the members more than the non-religious ones. In conclusion, you are less likely to haze someone with so much in common. National Jewish fraternities include Alpha Epsilon Pi, Zeta Beta Tau, and Sigma Alpha Mu. The national Jewish sororities are Alpha Epsilon Phi, Sigma Delta Tau, and Delta Phi Epsilon.

Even though I have told you how to avoid hazing, please realize that almost every chapter hazes in some way or another. Luckily, some of these things that are considered hazing by IFC standards aren't really that bad. These include, house clean-ups, interviews, kidnappings, running errands for actives, and many other things that are more of an inconvenience than real hazing.

What to Look For

There are many things to look for in choosing the correct fraternity or sorority. Here are the most important ones.

First, try to find out as much as possible about the chapter before rush. As I said, there is so much acting during the week of rush, it is impossible to get a real idea of what the chapters are like.

Second, try to see how the members treat each other. A close chapter won't be divided into clicks. If you see them ignoring each other in public, that is probably a good indication that their brotherhood or sisterhood is very weak. People who are bitter enemies will act like best of friends for the sake of rush.

Third, choose the chapter that you feel the most comfortable around. Don't choose a chapter just because they have a big house, the best looking little sisters, etc. Pick friends, not images or materialism. A good friend is a lot better to talk to than a Corvette.

Fourth, look at the costs as they vary from chapter to chapter. Once you get an idea of how much dues are, be sure to leave room in your wallet for t-shirts, formals, trips, paddles, and other Greek related items.

Conclusion

As I said before, fraternities and sororities have a lot to offer. Be careful, know your mental and financial limits, and have fun.

CHAPTER 9

ALCOHOL+ DRUGS

" The world is about three drinks behind."
- Humphry Bogart

"You are not drunk if you can lie on the floor without holding on."
- Dean Martin

Just like in the movie "Animal House," there is a lot of alcohol consumption in the college environment. The problem with drinking in college is that the focus is not put on how often you drink, but how much. There is absolutely no reason for you or anybody else to test your limits. Remember, alcohol can kill. Don't ever think you are a wimp or a lightweight because you can't drink like a fish. I'd rather be considered a lightweight than spend my night praying to the porcelain god or in a hospital getting my stomach pumped. Just like everything else, if you drink, drink responsibly.

Types of Drinkers

As you know, there are three types of drinkers. The first type of drinker is the social drinker. This type of drinking is the most common. Being a social drinker is perfectly acceptable as long as it is done responsibly. The signs of a social drinker are the following:

1. Drinks slowly.
2. Knows their limits.
3. Respects non-drinkers.

The next type of drinker is the problem drinker. The problem drinker usually drinks more in quantity and frequency than the social drinker. The signs of a problem drinker are:

1. Tries to solve problems by drinking.
2. Drinks at inappropriate times.
3. Experiences change in personality when drinking.
4. Causes problems for themselves and others
   around them.

The next type of drinker is the alcoholic. The alcoholic tends to center his or her life around their addiction. The signs of an alcoholic are:

1. Spends a lot of time either drinking or thinking
   about the next time they are going to get drunk.
2. Denies they have a drinking problem.
3. Experiences change in personality.
4. Causes problems with police, friends, or family.

Drinking Tips

If you decide to drink, here are some of my suggestions. First, don't drink to escape your problems. Alcohol is only a temporary fix for a more serious problem. Drinking for emotional reasons can easily lead to alcoholism.

Second, don't drink and drive. Remember, you are in college to get ahead in life, and a DUI can set you back financially, criminally, and emotionally. Usually when you go out, there will be at least one person that doesn't feel like drinking, so have that person drive.

Third, realize if there are any environmental factors that make you drink too much, you need to change them. Sometimes certain factors such as boredom along with certain people and places can make you drink more frequently and in quantity than you normally would.

Fourth, don't drink under pressure. If someone insists on you drinking, ask them why it is so important to them that you drink.

Last, but most important, alcohol and sex can be a deadly combination. The more intoxicated you are, the less likely you will feel the need to use protection. Just like the commercial says, "Get drunk, get stupid, get AIDS." If you get drunk, don't get stupid.

Conclusion

To sum up, drinking can be enjoyable if done responsibly. Follow the above suggestions, and you should avoid becoming a problem drinker or an alcoholic. In addition, having a wide range of activities that you enjoy helps take your mind off drinking. Remember, know the difference between fun and stupidity and watch out where you use your fake I.D.

Drugs

I will make this section short and sweet. Stay away from drugs! You are smart enough to know what a devastating effect they can have on your life. While some of you might have experimented with some of the lesser addictive drugs, you will find that in college, the real bad ones are more available. As I said before, you are in college to grow not revert. Be smart and just say no! Again, know the difference between fun and stupidity.

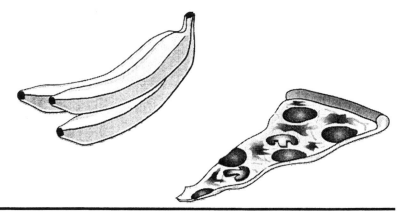

CHAPTER 10

NUTRITION

"Desserts remain for a moment or two in your
mouth and for the rest of your life on your hips."
    - Peg Bracken

I'm sure you have heard of the "Freshman 15."
While fifteen pounds seems like an exaggeration, if you
don't watch out, you will gain weight. Here are the most
common reasons why.

Dorm Food

Unfortunately, even though your parents pay a lot for
your college, the last thing the school uses the money for is
to feed you. Usually, the food in the dorms is mass pro-
cessed fried garbage. Needless to say, this type of food is
filled with fat and calories. Think of every trip to the cafe-
teria as a trip to McDonalds. Now, multiply that three
times a day, seven days a week.

Another problem with dorm food is not only is it loaded with fat and calories, but it is also usually all you can eat. Without self control, you can easily gorge down plates and plates of food without thinking of the damage being done to your body. Fortunately, some schools have realized this problem and have added lower fat foods to their menus.

Alcohol: the "Unknown Calories"

Even though we already discussed the effects of alcohol, we haven't talked about what it does to your diet. We have all grown up hearing "great taste - less filling," but how many times have you thought about what this means. Less filling means less calories along with feeling.

An average beer has roughly 200 calories. Please keep this in mind when you're evaluating your diet. Remember, a night of drinking can add more calories to your diet than a trip to McDonalds. Not only does alcohol add calories to your diet, but it also slows down your metabolism. Think twice before you over indulge in alcohol, and if you get the munchies after drinking, eat sensibly. Don't find the nearest fast food restaurant on your way home.

Snacking: the Ignored Calories

A part of college that we all go through is the over abundance of spare time. During this spare time, we often snack without realizing how many calories we are putting in our bodies. Things like pretzels, chips, and candy are loaded with fat and calories.

However, there are many things you can snack on without worrying. Almost every food company makes some sort of fat free snack. Try some of them and stick to them. Snacking should only be done to end hunger not boredom.

Keeping Kosher

The type, size, location, and Jewish population at your school will play a big role in your ability to keep kosher. Most state schools will provide vegetarian meals to try to accomodate students who keep kosher. Once you leave the dorms, keeping kosher will become easier. If you keep kosher, make sure you find out the options that your school will provide.

Solutions

Here are a few suggestions for good nutrition:

1. Get the meal plan that allows you the fewest meals per day. With a one or two meal a day program, you can easily find better tasting, more nutritious, and cheaper meals off campus or in the grocery store. The only thing to remember is not to replace junk with junk.

2. Buy a cookbook with quick and easy recipes. Many things can be prepared even though you are in the dorms. Most dorms either have microwaves or allow you to bring them. Another useful cooking appliance is the Snackmaster. This allows you to cook foods inexpensively that are fairly low in fat. Most dorms allow these types of cooking appliances. Check with your school before you buy one.

3. Look for fat contents on food packages. There are many college foods that are popular yet very fattening. The first is the popular Ramen noodles. A package of these contains more than 16 grams of fat. The next item, Chex Party Mix, is also loaded with salt and fat. Remember, when looking at fat contents, look for the serving size. Most companies put ridiculously low serving sizes to make it look like their product contains less fat and calories.

4. Watch out for fast food. Mostly all fast food restaurants have some type of nutritional information packet

about their food. Get one and find out how much fat you are consuming. Some good alternatives to traditional fast food restaurants are Subway and Boston Market.

Conclusion

I understand that occasionally time, money, and transportation can limit your ability to good nutrition. However, there are still many things you can do to better your nutrition regardless of your limits. Try your best to eat well, and the benefits will last a lifetime.

CHAPTER 11

EMOTIONS

"You may not know it, but at the far end of despair, there is a white clearing where one is almost happy."
    - Jean Anouilh

The worst part of college that you will have to adjust to is your range of emotions. As you have read in the previous chapters, there are many different aspects of college that will affect your emotions. There are two main areas you will probably experience: homesickness and depression.

Homesickness

Even if you absolutely enjoy your new friends, environment, and school, I guarantee that you will be a little homesick.

The reason everyone experiences homesickness is not so much because of missing home as it is a longing for your previous lifestyle, schedule, and stability. This is com mon when there is any abrupt change in your life.

Positive Ways to Deal with Homesickness

1. Don't go home every weekend. You eventually have to adjust to your new environment. By going home every weekend, you prolong the adjustment.

2. Don't run up huge phone bills by calling home. A call every few days is fine, but too many calls prolong your adjustment just like too many visits home.

3. Get involved in as many activities as you can. Staying busy not only keeps your mind off home but it also helps you meet people and adjust to your new environment.

4. Bring reminders of home such as pictures, movies, and other things that remind your family..

Depression

Unfortunately, you will probably deal with depression sometime during your college career. Since there are many reasons that cause depression, we will only discuss a few of them.

The most common type of depression comes from broken relationships. The first thing to remember when going through this change is that most of the time you are not depressed from losing the person, you are depressed from losing love and affection.

The next thing to remember about broken relationships is breaking the habit. When in a relationship, you begin to form many daily habits that revolve around your significant other. Remember, a habit can take as little as 21 days to form. Think of how many habits you can form during a long relationship. Just like smoking, habits from relationships take a while to break. The best way to break these habits is to keep busy with other activities until your depression ends.

The next thing to do is watch out for environmental reminders of your ex. Avoid restaurants, movie theaters, parks, and other places that you use to go. Don't go to these places until you are over the broken relationship.

Since most bookstores contain shelves full of books on broken relationships, I will strongly recommend one: *Letting Go*, by Dr. Zev Wanderer.

Another type of depression is what is known as general depression. This is usually depression due to things like loneliness and low self-confidence. There are many ways of dealing with these. Here are some of the best:

1. Find out exactly what you are depressed about. Many times, you will find that your problems are a lot less serious than you thought.

2. Change your lifestyle. Do things like working out, going to new places, buying new clothes, change your image, etc. Sometimes a "new you" can make you feel recharged and self-confident.

3. Try to do more enjoyable things such as going out more, spending more time with friends, and other activities that make you feel good.

4. Avoid excessively destructive behaviors such as alcoholism, anorexia, bulimia, promiscuity, and other behaviors that only lead to more serious problems down the road.

The next type of depression is the most tragic: the death of a loved one. As you enter your college years, you will find that family members start to enter their elderly years. In addition, with your vast network of friends at college, there is a chance that you will lose a loved one, friend, or an acquaintance. Since death is such a tragic thing, I only have two suggestions:

1. Get some sort of counseling. Most schools offer it free or for a very low charge. An option to general counseling is religious counseling. I'm sure that any Rabbi would be more than happy to counsel you in a time of need.

2. With death being a normal life event, there are many books on how to cope and accept it. One of the best is *On Death and Dying*, by Elizabeth Kubler-Ross.

Conclusion

Whatever type of depression you are going through, remember, life is full of ups and downs, and you always have to go on no matter what happens. Even though you might not see light at the end of the tunnel, it is there, I promise.

CHAPTER 12

SEX + STD's

" The human need for love and sex is made to bear the burden of all our bodily starvation for contact and sensation, all our creative starvation, all our need for social contact, and even our need to find some meaning in our lives."
- Dierdre English

I realize that if I were to tell you not to have sex under any circumstances, you probably would quit reading this book. Even though I will give you advice on how to make sex "safer," remember the only "safe" sex is no sex. While during your college years the environment supports and encourages sex, you will later realize that it is something you can easily live without.

Sex is a beautiful way of expressing love between two people. However, there are many reasons why you should limit or abstain from sexual activity. In the introduction of the book, I told you I wouldn't preach Judaism or morality, so I will only talk about one aspect of sexual behavior: sexually transmitted diseases (STD's).

STD's

Every year, approximately 12 million people contract a STD. Keep in mind, this number does not include cases that aren't reported. An estimated 63% of these 12 million were people under the age of 25. One study I recently read came up with the estimation that 10% of all college students have contracted a STD sometime in their life. The next study I found stated that rate is now as high as 20%. The question then becomes how much do you want to play with statistics? Personally, I like to play with statistics like this as often as I play Russian Roulette.

As you know, anybody can contract STD's no matter what their sex, race, religion, creed, age or any other social or biological factor may be. Even though you don't hear about high numbers of Jews contracting STD's, don't think that we are immune. I guarantee that some of those 12 million were Jewish, and possibly someone you know.

You might think that all these 12 million people that contracted STD's were irresponsible, sleazy, or weren't careful, but you're wrong. No matter how careful you are or how much you think you know someone, something un-planned could easily happen. If you think you know and can trust someone enough not to use any protection, here are two stories of people I know affected by STD's.

The first story is about a girl I met that we will call "Mary." She was an middle to upper class college student with a boyfriend for over two years. Her life was seemingly perfect until her prince dropped a bomb on her. According to his story, one night he had an urge to go to a gay bar.

Finding this club and life enjoyable, he picked up another man, took him home, and had sex. Not only was he unfaithful for the first time, he also contracted HIV . After he informed "Mary" of this, she then had to spend the next six months of her life getting an HIV test every week and praying that she hadn't contracted it from him during the few times they had unprotected sex. Luckily, after six months of testing, she tested negative. Needless to say, now she is a very strong supporter of abstinence. I think you would be too if sex had almost cost you your life.

The next story is about a girl I know that we will call "Susan." Like "Mary" she too was a college student involved in a long relationship that couldn't have been stronger. She was taking the pill as contraception and really never doubted her boyfriend's love. That is, until he cheated on her and gave her herpes. She now has to spend the rest of her life taking medication and treating reoccurring flare-ups.

The "Myth" of the Condom

Condoms are highly effective in reducing the spread of STD's. If you are going to have sex, always use a condom no matter what - **no exceptions.** Next to abstinence, condoms are the next safest alternative. Unfortunately, condoms are far from being safe, as they are just "safer" than any other form of birth control. Realize that most of the STD's are transmitted by blood, fluid, or skin contact. A condom does not cover every inch of your skin, therefore, it is easily possible to contract a STD when using a condom. Furthermore, condoms can break or fall off leaving you without any protection at all. You will then find out how quick your safe sex can become a death sentence. The idea that if you wear a condom you won't catch anything is far from the truth.

Other Forms of Birth Control

Keep in mind that birth control is exactly what it says, and not STD control. While pregnancy is a major concern of many women, so should STD's. Obviously, if you are worried about pregnancy, you aren't practicing the "safer" sex that we have already talked about.

Remember, all birth controls have two failure rates. The first failure rate is called the lowest observed failure rate. This means the least likely they have been known to fail. The second failure rate is called the typical failure rate. This means how often they usually fail. Keep in mind that even though some birth controls have extremely low failure rates, nothing is 100% effective.

Remember, besides medical reasons, other forms of birth control are only useful as backups for condoms.Since I am not a medical doctor and there are many forms of birth control, I will leave this decision to you and your doctor.

Conclusion

Unfortunately, there are too many STD's for me to discuss. There are over eight major STD's, and each of them have different ways of contraction, symptoms, treatments, and cures (if available). Remember, once again, abstinence is the only way to totally prevent contracting a STD.

While sex is a concern and urge to most college students, remember that the choices you make now, you will have to live with the rest of your life. To conclude, let me first say that while you might meet the perfect guy or girl, nobody is worth contracting a STD. If you are going to play the game, be ready to accept the consequences.

She said
no, but
she meant
yes

CHAPTER 13

Date Rape

"Rapes are rarely committed by isolated maniacs;
they are more often brutal acts carried out by ordi-
narily perfectly "normal" people."
- Author Unknown

Unfortunately, this is a subject that needs to be in any
college survival guide. I say unfortunately not because I
don't want to inform you about date rape, I just personally
find it unfortunate that some college level students still don't
know what the word "no" means. It seems strange that some
of them can work complex calculus problems, but still can't
understand that *no means no*.

Let me first say that I am not an expert on date rape
nor should this book be your only guide to preventing it.
Almost every college campus puts on seminars and self
defense classes to help prevent date rape. It is imperative that
you take at least one. Remember, it is estimated that roughly

1 in 4 college women will become the victim of date rape. Going to a rape prevention seminar can be your first step to avoid being that 1 victim.

Definition

There are two ways to define date rape: the legal way and the textbook way. The legal way is the hardest to define. Different states have different definitions of what constitutes date rape. The textbook way, defines it as "nonconcensual sex between adults who know each other."

Regardless of what definition you want to follow, remember the key word: *consent*. Anything after the word *no*, or any action that shows nonconsent is grounds for criminal prosecution.

Avoiding Date Rape

First of all, there is no absolute way to pick a guy out of a crowd who date rapes. He could be the big strong football player, as he could also be the quiet little bookworm. Realize that you can always take measures to prevent date rape, but aside from not dating at all, there is no absolute way to prevent it. The only thing you can do is to watch for certain behaviors and characteristics and to learn rape prevention and self defense.

Until you go to a seminar where date rape is talked about extensively, here are some general characteristics to watch out for in guys that you meet. These main areas come from *Acquaintance Rape, the Hidden Crime,* by Andrea Parrot.

The first area is "sexual entitlement." This involves the sexual behavior of the person. This includes unwanted touching, conversation that is inappropriately sexual in nature, or making excessive sexual or abusive remarks regarding women and their bodies.

The second area is power and control. These behaviors include showing excessive competitiveness, being a "bad loser," using intimidating body language, and game playing.

The next area is hostility and anger. These behaviors include showing a quick temper, blaming others when things go wrong, and transforming emotions into anger.

The last area is acceptance of interpersonal violence. These behaviors include using threats in displays of anger, using violence in borderline situations, and approving or justifying observed violence. Watch out for every one of these characteristics. If you meet someone that displays them, avoid them like the plague.

Unfortunately, as a Freshman woman, you will be the prime target of the "scammers." They know that you are new to the school, eager to "party," vulnerable, and wanting to find your first college romance. I promise you these jerks will try to capitalize on this. Here are some suggestions of what to look out for until you attend your rape prevention seminar.

1. Don't fall for lures. There are hundreds of ways that guys will try to lure you into their dorm rooms or apartments. It can be anything from "studying together" to "cooking dinner." Don't fall for these no matter how much you like the person. After all, what can't he do at a restaurant, club, or the library?

2. Avoid alcohol on dates. Remember, 90% of all date rapes have one thing in common: alcohol.

3. If you go to parties, stay around the crowd . Don't go upstairs or into anyone's room.

4. Don't just go out with anybody who asks. Always get to know someone before you go out with them. Even though it doesn't work 100% of the time, it helps.

5. When going out on dates, clearly define your limits. If any sexual suggestions or any "change of plans" are made, be strong, state your opposition, and say no.

Conclusion

To conclude, always be on your toes when it comes to dating. Remember, your first step to preventing date rape is learning about it. Go to rape prevention seminars, and I promise it will be the most useful "class" you will ever attend.

CONCLUSION

I hope you have enjoyed reading *Staying Jewish and Surviving College* as much as I enjoyed writing it. It has been a pleasure to take on such a great mitzvah of providing a resource to help guide the Jewish student during such an important time. If you take one lesson from this book and it has a positive impact on your life, my intent for writing this book will have been fulfilled.

As you will find out, this is a time of maturity and the final transition from adolescence into adulthood. There are many choices you will make over the next few years that can have a large impact on your years to come. In keeping with the general message of this book, let this be a time where you not only become more responsible as an adult, but also as a Jew. The rewards for taking on this meaningful responsibility will surely bring you happiness and success in the future. I hope you realize that while you are in one stage of your life, you are planning for the next. When you're in high school you plan for college. When you are in college, you plan for the rest of your life. If you plan on living a Jewish life, make Jewish decisions now. The most important decision you can make is to date and marry within the faith. As I mentioned earlier in the chapter on picking your dates, the feeling of being a bride or groom in a Jewish wedding is an indescribable feeling.

I hope you enjoy your time at college and that it is everything you expect it to be. Please feel free to contact me with any additional questions or comments you might have. I am always open to suggestions regarding the contents of this book. There is a distinct difference between the original version and its' present form because my readers took the time to tell me what they thought.

Take care, be well, and God Bless you.

PRAYERS
FOR
SPECIAL
OCCASIONS

The following is a collection of prayers* for special occasions. For a complete service of prayers, please refer to a Siddur.

*exerts from United Jewish Appeal (now United Jewish Communities) Book of Songs and Blessings, Sabbath and Festival Prayer Book, Gates of Prayer, To Be A Jew, and The Complete Siddur for Davkawriter.

SHABBAT PRAYERS

Lighting Candles

בָּרוּךְ אַתָּה יְיָ אֱלֹהֵינוּ מֶלֶךְ הָעוֹלָם. אֲשֶׁר קִדְּשָׁנוּ
בְּמִצְוֹתָיו, וְצִוָּנוּ לְהַדְלִיק נֵר שֶׁל שַׁבָּת.

Baruch Ata Adonai, Eloheinu melech ha-olam, asher kidshanu b' mitzvotav v'tzivanu l'hadlik ner shel Shabbat.

Blessed art Thou, Lord our God, King of the universe who has sanctified us with His commandments and ordained that we kindle the Sabbath light.

Shalom Aleichem

שָׁלוֹם עֲלֵיכֶם, מַלְאֲכֵי הַשָּׁרֵת, מַלְאֲכֵי עֶלְיוֹן, מִמֶּלֶךְ
מַלְכֵי הַמְּלָכִים, הַקָּדוֹשׁ בָּרוּךְ הוּא:
בּוֹאֲכֶם לְשָׁלוֹם, מַלְאֲכֵי הַשָּׁלוֹם, מַלְאֲכֵי עֶלְיוֹן,
מִמֶּלֶךְ מַלְכֵי הַמְּלָכִים, הַקָּדוֹשׁ בָּרוּךְ הוּא:
בָּרְכ וּנִי לְשָׁלוֹם, מַלְאֲכֵי הַשָּׁלוֹם, מַלְאֲכֵי עֶלְיוֹן,
מִמֶּלֶךְ מַלְכֵי הַמְּלָכִים, הַקָּדוֹשׁ בָּרוּךְ הוּא:
צֵאתְכֶם לְשָׁלוֹם, מַלְאֲכֵי הַשָּׁלוֹם, מַלְאֲכֵי עֶלְיוֹן,
מִמֶּלֶךְ מַלְכֵי הַמְּלָכִים, הַקָּדוֹשׁ בָּרוּךְ הוּא:

Shalom aleichem malachei hashareit malachei elyon, mimelech malchei ham'lachim, hakadosh baruch hu.

Bo-achem l'shalom malachei hashalom, malachei elyon mimelech malchei ham'lachim, hakadosh baruch hu

Barchuni l'shalom malachei hashalom malachei elyon mimelech malchei ham'lahim, hakadosh baruch hu

Tzeitchem l'shalom malachei hashalom, malachei elyon, mimelech malchei ham'lachim, hakadosh baruch hu

Peace be unto you ministering angels, messengers of the Most High. The King of Kings, the Holy One, blessed be He.
May your coming be in peace, messengers of peace, messengers of the Most High. The King of Kings, the Holy One, blessed be He.

Bless me with peace, messengers of peace, messengers of the Most High. The King of Kings, the Holy One, blessed be He.
May your departure be in peace, messengers of peace, messengers of the Most High. The King of Kings, the Holy One, blessed be He.

L'cha dodi

לְכָה דוֹדִי לִקְרַאת כַּלָּה. פְּנֵי שַׁבָּת נְקַבְּלָה:
לִקְרַאת שַׁבָּת לְכוּ וְנֵלְכָה. כִּי הִיא מְקוֹר הַבְּרָכָה.
מֵרֹאשׁ מִקֶּדֶם נְסוּכָה. סוֹף מַעֲשֶׂה בְּמַחֲשָׁבָה תְּחִלָּה:

הִתְעוֹרְרִי הִתְעוֹרְרִי. כִּי בָא אוֹרֵךְ קוּמִי אוֹרִי. עוּרִי
עוּרִי שִׁיר דַּבֵּרִי. כְּבוֹד יְיָ עָלַיִךְ נִגְלָה: לכה

בּוֹאִי בְשָׁלוֹם עֲטֶרֶת בַּעְלָהּ. גַּם בְּשִׂמְחָה וּבְצָהֳלָה.
תּוֹךְ אֱמוּנֵי עַם סְגֻלָּה. בּוֹאִי כַלָּה, בּוֹאִי כַלָּה: לכה:

L'cha dodi likrat kala p'nei Shabbat n'kabla.

*Likrat Shabbat l'chu v'nelcha, ki hi m'kor
habracha,*
*Merosh mikedem n'sucha sof ma'aseh
b'machshava t'chila.*

*Hitoreri hitoreri, , ki va orech kumi ori
Uri uri, shir daberi, k'vod Adonai alayich nigla.*

*Bo'i v'shalom ateret ba'la, gam b'simcha
uvtzohola,*
Toch emunei am s'gula, Bo'i chala bo'i chala.

Come, my friend, the Bride to meet, the Holy
Shabbat let us greet.

To greet Shabbat now let us go,
Source of blessing, it has ever been so.
Conceived before life on earth began,
Last in God's work, first in His plan.

Arise, arise, for your light has come,
The dawn has broken, the night is gone.
Awake, awake, and joyously sing;
Heavenly glory to you He did bring.

Come now, Shabbat, the day divine,
Come in joy, let your brightness shine.
Come to the people which greets you with pride.
Come in peace, Shabbat bride.

She-ma

שְׁמַע | יִשְׂרָאֵל, יְיָ | אֱלֹהֵינוּ, יְיָ | אֶחָד:

She-ma Yisrael; Adonai Eloheinu, Adonai Echad

Hear o Israel, the Lord is our God, the Lord is One

בָּרוּךְ שֵׁם כְּבוֹד מַלְכוּתוֹ לְעוֹלָם וָעֶד.

Baruch sheim k'vod malchuto l'olam va-ed.

Blessed be the name of His glorious majesty for
ever and ever.

וְאָהַבְתָּ אֵת יְיָ | אֱלֹהֶיךָ, בְּכָל-לְבָבְךָ, וּבְכָל-נַפְשְׁךָ,
וּבְכָל-מְאֹדֶךָ. וְהָיוּ הַדְּבָרִים הָאֵלֶּה, אֲשֶׁר | אָ‎נֹכִי
מְצַוְּךָ הַיּוֹם, עַל-לְבָבֶךָ: וְשִׁנַּנְתָּם לְבָנֶיךָ, וְדִבַּרְתָּ
בָּם בְּשִׁבְתְּךָ בְּבֵיתֶךָ, וּבְלֶכְתְּךָ בַדֶּרֶךְ וּ‎, בְשָׁכְבְּךָ,
וּבְקוּמֶךָ. וּקְשַׁרְתָּם לְאוֹת | עַל-יָדֶךָ, וְהָיוּ לְטֹטָפֹת
בֵּין | עֵינֶיךָ, וּכְתַבְתָּם | עַל מְזֻזוֹת בֵּיתֶךָ וּבִשְׁעָרֶיךָ:

*V'a-havta et Adonai elohecha b'chol l'vavcha
uv-chol naf'sh'cha uv-chol m'odecha. V'hayu
hadvarim ha-aileh asher anochi m'tzav-cha
ha-yom al l'vavecha, v'sheenantam l'vanecha
v'dee-barta bam, b'sheev-t'cha b'vaitecha
uv-lech-t'cha va-derech, uv-shach-b'cha
uv-kumecha. Uk-shartam l'ot al yadecha, v'hayu
l'totafot bayn aynecha uch-tavtam al mezuzot
baytecha u-vish-arecha.*

And thou shalt love thy Lord thy God with all thy
heart, with all thy soul, and with all thy might. And
these words which I command thee this day shall
be in thy heart. Thou shalt teach them diligently
unto thy children, speak of them when thy sittest in
thy house, when thou walkest by the way, when
thou liest down and when thou risest up. And thou
shalt bind them for a sign upon thy hand, and they
shall be for frontlets between thine eyes. And thou
shalt inscribe them on the door posts of thy house
and upon thy gates.

Mi cha-mo-cha

מִי כָמֹכָה בָּאֵלִים יְיָ, מִי כָּמֹכָה נֶאְדָּר בַּקֹּדֶשׁ, נוֹרָא
תְהִלֹּת,עֹשֵׂה פֶ לֶא: מַלְכוּתְךָ רָאוּ בָנֶיךָ,בּוֹקֵ עַ יָם
לִפְנֵי מֹשֶׁה, זֶה אֵלִי עָנוּ וְאָמְרוּ: יְיָ יִמְלֹךְ לְעוֹלָם
וָעֶד. וְנֶאֱמַר: כִּי פָדָה יְיָ אֶת יַעֲקֹב, וּגְאָלוֹ מִיַּד חָזָק
מִמֶּנּוּ.בָּרוּךְ אַתָּה יְיָ, גָּאַל יִשְׂרָאֵל:

Mi cha-mo-cha ba-ei-lim, Adonai?
Mi cha-mo-cha ne-dar ba-ko-desh,
no-ra te-hi-lot, o-sei fe-leh?
Mal-chu-te-cha ra-u va-necha,
bokei-a yam li-fenei Mo-sheh;
"Zeh Ei-li" a-nu ve-a-me-ru.
"Adonai yim-loch le-o-lam va-ed."
Ve-ne-e-mar: "Ki fa-da Adonai et Ya-a-kov,
u-ge-a-lo mi-yad cha-zak mi-me-nu."
Ba-ruch Ata Adonai, ga-al Yisrael.

Who is like unto Thee, o Lord, among the mighty?
Who is like unto Thee, glorious in holiness,

Revered in praises, doing wonders?
This is my God! they exclaimed, and said:
"The Lord shall reign for ever and ever."
Blessed art Thou, O Lord, redeemer of Israel.

V'shamru

וְשָׁמְרוּ בְנֵי יִשְׂרָאֵל אֶת הַשַּׁבָּת, לַעֲשׂוֹת אֶת הַשַּׁבָּת
לְדֹרֹתָם בְּרִית עוֹלָם: בֵּינִי וּבֵין בְּנֵי יִשְׂרָאֵל אוֹת
הִיא לְעוֹלָם, כִּי שֵׁשֶׁת יָמִים עָשָׂה יְיָ אֶת הַשָּׁמַיִם
וְאֶת הָאָרֶץ, וּבַיּוֹם הַשְּׁבִיעִי שָׁבַת וַיִּנָּפַשׁ.

Ve-sham-ru ve-nei Yisrael et ha-Shabat,
la-a-sot et ha-Shabat le-doro-tam bei-rit olam.
Bei-ni uvein be-nai Yisrael ot hi le-o-lam.
Ki shei-shet ya-mim a-sa Adonai et hasha-ma-yim
ve-et ha-a-rets, u v'yom ha-she-vi-i sha-vat
va-yi-na-fash.

The people of Israel shall keep the Sabbath,
observing the Sabbath in every generation as a
covenant for all time. It is a sign for ever and ever
between Me and the people of Israel, for in six
days the Eternal God made heaven and earth, and
on the seventh day He rested from his labors.

Kiddush

סַבְרִי מָרָנָן וְרַבָּנָן וְרַבּוֹתַי.

בָּרוּךְ אַתָּה יְיָ אֱלֹהֵינוּ מֶלֶךְ הָעוֹלָם, בּוֹרֵא פְּרִי הַגָּפֶן.

בָּרוּךְ אַתָּה יְיָ אֱלֹהֵינוּ מֶלֶךְ הָעוֹלָם, אֲשֶׁר קִדְּשָׁנוּ
בְּמִצְוֹתָיו וְרָצָה בָנוּ, וְשַׁבַּת קָדְשׁוֹ בְּאַהֲבָה וּבְרָצוֹן

הִנְחִילָנוּ זִכָּרוֹן לְמַעֲשֵׂה בְרֵאשִׁית, כִּי הוּא יוֹם תְּחִלָּה
לְמִקְרָאֵי קֹדֶשׁ, זֵכֶר לִיצִיאַת מִצְרָיִם, כִּי בָנוּ בָחַרְתָּ
וְאוֹתָנוּ קִדַּשְׁתָּ מִכָּל הָעַמִּים, וְשַׁבַּת קָדְשְׁךָ בְּאַהֲבָה
וּבְרָצוֹן הִנְחַלְתָּנוּ. בָּרוּךְ אַתָּה יְיָ, מְקַדֵּשׁ הַשַּׁבָּת.

Savrei maranan v'rabotai:
Baruch Ata Adonai, Eloheinu melech ha-olam,
borei pri hagafen.

Blessed art Thou, Lord our God, King of the
universe, Creator of the fruit of the vine.

Baruch Ata Adonai, Eloheinu melech
ha-olam,asher kidshanu b'mitzvotav v'ratza vanu,
v'Shabat kodsho b'ahava uvratzon hinchilanu,
zicaron l'ma-asei v'reishit. Ki hu yom t'chila
l'mikra-ei kodesh, zecher litziyat mitzrayim. Ki
vanu vacharta v'otanu kidashta mikol ha-amim,
v'Shabbat kodh'cha b'ahava uv-ratzon
hinchaltanu, BaruchAta Adonai, m'kadesh
haShabbat.

Blessed art Thou, Lord our God, King of the
universe, who has taught us the way of holiness
through Mitzvot. Lovingly Thou hast favored us
with the gift of Thy holy Shabbat as our
inheritance, a reminder of creation, first among the
sacred days which recall the Exodus from Egypt.
Thou hast chosen us of all peoples for thy service,
and thou hast given us a sacred purpose in life. In
loving favor, Thou hast given us Thy holy Shabbat
as a heritage. Blessed art Thou, O Lord, who
hallows the Shabbat.

Kaddish

יִתְגַּדַּל וְיִתְקַדַּשׁ שְׁמֵהּ רַבָּא. בְּעָלְמָא דִּי בְרָא
כִרְעוּתֵהּ, וְיַמְלִיךְ מַלְכוּתֵהּ בְּחַיֵּיכוֹן וּבְיוֹמֵיכוֹן וּבְחַיֵּי
דְכָל בֵּית יִשְׂרָאֵל. בַּעֲגָלָא וּבִזְמַן קָרִיב, וְאִמְרוּ אָמֵן:
יְהֵא שְׁמֵהּ רַבָּא מְבָרַךְ לְעָלַם וּלְעָלְמֵי עָלְמַיָּא:
יִתְבָּרַךְ וְיִשְׁתַּבַּח, וְיִתְפָּאַר וְיִתְרוֹמַם וְיִתְנַשֵּׂא וְיִתְהַדָּר
וְיִתְעַלֶּה וְיִתְהַלָּל שְׁמֵהּ דְּקֻדְשָׁא בְּרִיךְ הוּא לְעֵלָּא מִן
כָּל בִּרְכָתָא וְשִׁירָתָא, תֻּשְׁבְּחָתָא וְנֶחֱמָתָא, דַּאֲמִירָן
בְּעָלְמָא, וְאִמְרוּ אָמֵן:
יְהֵא שְׁלָמָא רַבָּא מִן שְׁמַיָּא וְחַיִּים טוֹבִים עָלֵינוּ וְעַל
כָּל יִשְׂרָאֵל, וְאִמְרוּ אָמֵן:
עֹשֶׂה שָׁלוֹם בִּמְרוֹמָיו הוּא בְּרַחֲמָיו יַעֲשֶׂה שָׁלוֹם
עָלֵינוּ וְעַל כָּל יִשְׂרָאֵל, וְאִמְרוּ אָמֵן:

Yitgadal v'yitkadash sh'mei raba. B'alma di v'ra
chirutei, v'yamlich malchutei b'cha-yeichon
uv-yomeichon, uv-cha-yei d'chol bet Yisrael,
ba'agala u-vizman kariv, v'imru Amein.
Y'hei sh'mei raba m'vorach l'alam ul-almei
almaya.
Yitbarach v'yishtabach v'yitpa'ar v'yitromam
v'yitnasei, v'yithadad v'yitaleh v'yit halal sh'mei
d'kudsha b'rich Hu. L'eilah min kol birchata
v'shirashta, tushb'chata v'nechemata, da'amiran
b'alma v'imru Amein.
Y'hei sh'lama raba min sh'maya, v'chayim aleinu
v'al kol Yisrael, v'imru Amein.
Oseh shalom bim'romav, hu ya'aseh shlalom
aleinnu v'al kol Yisrael, v/imru Amein.

Exalted and hollowed be God's great name In this world of his creation.
May His will be fulfilled and His soveignty revealed in the days of your lifetime and the life of the whole house of Israel speedily and soon, and say, Amen.

Be His great name blessed forever, Yea to all eternity.

Be the name of the most Holy One blessed, praised and honored, extolled and glorified, adored and exhalted supremely. Blessed be He, beyond all blessings and hymns, praises and consolations that may be uttered in this world. And say, Amen.

May peace abundant descend from heaven with life for us and Israel, and say, Amen.

May He who creates the harmony of the spheres create peace for us and all Israel, and say, Amen.

Adon Olam

אֲדוֹן עוֹלָם אֲשֶׁר מָלַךְ,   בְּטֶרֶם כָּל יְצִיר נִבְרָא:

לְעֵת נַעֲשָׂה בְחֶפְצוֹ כֹּל,   אֲזַי מֶלֶךְ שְׁמוֹ נִקְרָא:

וְאַחֲרֵי כִּכְלוֹת הַכֹּל,   לְבַדּוֹ יִמְלוֹךְ נוֹרָא.

וְהוּא הָיָה, וְהוּא הֹוֶה,   וְהוּא יִהְיֶה, בְּתִפְאָרָה.

וְהוּא אֶחָד וְאֵין שֵׁנִי,   לְהַמְשִׁיל לוֹ לְהַחְבִּירָה.

בְּלִי רֵאשִׁית בְּלִי תַכְלִית,   וְלוֹ הָעֹז וְהַמִּשְׂרָה.

וְהוּא אֵלִי וְחַי גֹּאֲלִי,   וְצוּר חֶבְלִי בְּעֵת צָרָה.

וְהוּא נִסִּי וּמָנוֹס לִי,   מְנָת כּוֹסִי בְּיוֹם אֶקְרָא.

בְּעֵת אִישָׁן וְאָעִירָה.   בְּיָדוֹ אַפְקִיד רוּחִי,

יְיָ לִי וְלֹא אִירָא.   וְעִם רוּחִי גְּוִיָּתִי

Adon olam, asher mlach,	b'terem kol y'tzir nivra
L'et nasa v'cheftzo kol	azai melech sh'mo nikra
Vacharei kichlot ha-kol	l'vado yimloch nora
Vhu ha-ya, v'hu hoveh	v'hu yih-yeh b'tifara
Vhu echad, v'ein sheni	l'hamshil lo l'hachbira
B'li reishit, b'li tachlit	v'lo haoz v'hamisra
V'hu eeili v'chai go-ali	v'tzur chevli b'et tzara
V'hu nisi umanos li	m'nat kosi b'yom ekra
B'yado afkid ruchi	b'et ishan v'a-ira
V'im ruchi g'viyati	Adonai li v'lo ira.

Lord of the world, He reigned alone, while yet the universe was naught, When by His will things were wrought, then first His sovereign name was known.

And when the all shall cease to be, in dread lone splendor He shall reign. He was, He is, He shall remain in glorious eternity.

For He is one, no second shares His nature or His loneliness; Unending and beginningless all strength is His, all sway he bears. He is the living God to save, my rock while sorrow's toils endure, my banner and my stronghold sure, the cup of life whenever I crave. I place my soul within His palm before I sleep as when I wake, and though my body I forsake, rest in the Lord in fearless calm.

Yigdal

יִגְדַּל אֱלֹהִים חַי וְיִשְׁתַּבַּח, נִמְצָא, וְאֵין עֵת אֶל
מְצִיאוּתוֹ:

אֶחָד וְאֵין יָחִיד כְּיִחוּדוֹ, נֶעְלָם, וְגַם אֵין סוֹף
לְאַחְדוּתוֹ:

אֵין לוֹ דְמוּת הַגּוּף וְאֵינוֹ גוּף, לֹא נַעֲרוֹךְ אֵלָיו
קְדֻשָּׁתוֹ:

קַדְמוֹן לְכָל דָּבָר אֲשֶׁר נִבְרָא, רִאשׁוֹן וְאֵין
רֵאשִׁית לְרֵאשִׁיתוֹ:

הִנּוֹ אֲדוֹן עוֹלָם, לְכָל נוֹצָר. יוֹרֶה גְדֻלָּתוֹ
וּמַלְכוּתוֹ:

שֶׁפַע נְבוּאָתוֹ נְתָנוֹ, אֶל אַנְשֵׁי סְגֻלָּתוֹ
וְתִפְאַרְתּוֹ:

לֹא קָם בְּיִשְׂרָאֵל כְּמֹשֶׁה עוֹד, נָבִיא וּמַבִּיט
אֶת תְּמוּנָתוֹ:

תּוֹרַת אֱמֶת נָתַן לְעַמּוֹ, אֵל, עַל יַד נְבִיאוֹ
נֶאֱמַן בֵּיתוֹ:

לֹא יַחֲלִיף הָאֵל וְלֹא יָמִיר דָּתוֹ. לְעוֹלָמִים,
לְזוּלָתוֹ:

צוֹפֶה וְיוֹדֵ עַ סְתָרֵינוּ, מַבִּיט לְסוֹף דָּבָר
בְּקַדְמָתוֹ:

גּוֹמֵל לְאִישׁ חֶסֶד כְּמִפְעָלוֹ, נוֹתֵן לְרָשָׁע רָע
כְּרִשְׁעָתוֹ:

יִשְׁלַח לְקֵץ הַיָּמִין מְשִׁיחֵנוּ, לִפְדּוֹת מְחַכֵּי קֵץ יְשׁוּעָתוֹ:

מֵתִים יְחַיֶּה אֵל בְּרוֹב חַסְדּוֹ, בָּרוּךְ עֲדֵי עַד שֵׁם תְּהִלָּתוֹ:

Yig-dal E-lo-him chai ve-yish-ta-bach,
nim-tsa ve-ein eit el me-tsi-u-to.
Echad ve-ein ya-chid keyi-chu-do, ne-lam ve-gam
ein sof le-ach-du-to.
Ein lo de-mut ha-guf ve-ein-o guf,
lo na-a-roch eilav ke-du-shato.
Kadmon le-chol da-var asher niv-ra,
ri-shon ve-ein rei-shit le-rei-shi-to.
Hi-no adom o-lam, le-chol no-tsar
yo-reh ge-du-la-to u-mal-chu-to.
She-fa ne-vu-a-to ne-ta-no,
el a-ne-shei se-gu-la-to ve-tif-ar-to.
Lo kam be-yis-rael ke-mo-sheh od
na-vi u-ma-bit et te-mu-na-to
Torat e-memt na-tan lea-mo El,
al yad ne-vi-o ne-e-man beito.
Lo ya-cha-lif hael, velo ya-mir da-to, le-o-la-mim
le-zu-la-to.
Tso feh ve-yo-dei-a se-ta-rei-nu,
ma-bit le-sof da-var bekad-ma-to.
Go-meil le-ish che-sed ke-mif-alo,
no-tein le-rash-a ra ke-risha-to.
Yish-lach le-keits ya-min meshe-ha-nu
Lif-dot me-ha-kay ketz ye-sho-a-to.
May-tim ye-ha el be-rov has-do
ba-ruh a-dei ad sheim te-hi-la-to.

The living God O magnify and bless,
Transcending time and here eternally.

One Being, yet unique in unity;
A mystery of Oneness, measureless.

Lo! form or body He has none, and man
No semblance of His holiness can frame.

Before Creation's dawn He was the same;
The first to be, though never He began.

He is the world's and every creatures Lord;
His rule and majesty are manifest,

And through His chosen, glorious sons exprest
In prophecies that through their lips are poured.

Yet never like to Moses rose a seer,
Permitted glimpse behind the veil divine.

This faithful Prince of God's prophetic line
Received the Law of Truth for Israel's ear.

Thy Law God gave' He will never amend,
Nor ever by another Law replace.

Our secret things are spread before His face;
In all beginnings He beholds the end.

The saint's reward He measures to his meed;
The sinner reaps the harvest of his ways.

Messiah He will send at end of days,
And all the faithful to salvation lead.

God will the dead again to life restore
In his abundance of almighty love.

Then blessed be His name, all names above,
And let His praise resound forevermore.

Hamotzi

בָּרוּךְ אַתָּה יְיָ, אֱלֹהֵינוּ מֶלֶךְ הָעוֹלָם, הַמּוֹצִיא לֶחֶם מִן
הָאָרֶץ.

*BaruchAta Adonai, Eloheinu melech ha-olam,
hamotzi lechem min ha-aretz.*

Blessed art Thou, King of the universe, who brings
forth bread from the earth.

Havdalah

הִנֵּה אֵל יְשׁוּעָתִי, אֶבְטַח וְלֹא אֶפְחָד, כִּי עָזִּי וְזִמְרָת
יָהּ יְיָ, וַיְהִי לִי לִישׁוּעָה: וּשְׁאַבְתֶּם מַיִם בְּשָׂשׂוֹן
מִמַּעַיְנֵי הַיְשׁוּעָה: לַיְיָ הַיְשׁוּעָה עַל עַמְּךָ בִרְכָתֶךָ
סֶּלָה: יְיָ צְבָאוֹת עִמָּנוּ מִשְׂגָּב לָנוּ אֱלֹהֵי יַעֲקֹב סֶלָה:
יְיָ צְבָאוֹת אַשְׁרֵי אָדָם בֹּטֵחַ בָּךְ: יְיָ הוֹשִׁיעָה הַמֶּלֶךְ
יַעֲנֵנוּ בְיוֹם קָרְאֵנוּ: לַיְהוּדִים הָיְתָה אוֹרָה וְשִׂמְחָה
וְשָׂשׂוֹן וִיקָר: כֵּן תִּהְיֶה לָּנוּ, כּוֹס יְשׁוּעוֹת אֶשָּׂא.
וּבְשֵׁם יְיָ אֶקְרָא:

*Hinei Eil yeshuati, evtach v'lo efchad, ki ozi
v'zimrat yah Adonai, vay-hi li lishua. Ush-avtem
mayim b'sason mima-y'nei ha-y'shua. Ladonai
ha-y'shua al amcha birchatecha sela. Adonai
tz'va-ot imanu, misgav lanu Elohei Ya'akov sela.
Adonai tz'va-ot , ashrei adam bote-ach bach.*

Adonai hoshia, hamelech ya'aneinu v'yom koreinu. La-y'hudim ha-y'ta orav'simcha v'sason vikar. Ken tih-yeh lanu. Kos y'shuot es, uv-shem Adonai ekra.

Behold, God is my salvation, I trust and am not afraid; for the Lord Eternal is my strength and song, and He is become my liberation. Therefore with joy shall you draw water from the wells of salvation. Thine, O Lord, is salvation; Thy blessing on Thy people. Selah. Lord of hosts, be with us, God of Jacob, be our high refuge. Selah. Lord of hosts, happy is the man who trusts in Thee. Lord, save us, may the King answer us on the day when we call. The Jews had light and gladness, joy and honor. So may it be with us. I will lift up the cup of salvation and proclaim the name of the Lord.

סַבְרִי מָרָנָן וְרַבָּנָן וְרַבּוֹתַי:

בָּרוּךְ אַתָּה יְיָ, אֱלֹהֵֽינוּ מֶֽלֶךְ הָעוֹלָם, בּוֹרֵא פְּרִי הַגָּֽפֶן.

Baruch Ata Adonai, Eloheinu melech ha-olam, borei pri hagafen.

Blessed art Thou, Lord our God, King of the universe, who creates the fruit of the vine.

Before the spice box

בָּרוּךְ אַתָּה יְיָ, אֱלֹהֵינוּ מֶלֶךְ הָעוֹלָם, בּוֹרֵא מִינֵי בְשָׂמִים:

Baruch Ata Adonai, Eloheinu melech ha-olam, borei minei v'samim.

Blessed art Thou, Lord our God, King of the universe, who creates the various spices.

Holding fingers in the light of the candle

בָּרוּךְ אַתָּה יְיָ, אֱלֹהֵינוּ מֶלֶךְ הָעוֹלָם, בּוֹרֵא מְאוֹרֵי הָאֵשׁ:

Baruch Ata Adonai, Eloheinu melech ha-olam, borei m'orei ha-esh.
Blessed art Thou, Lord our God, King of the universe, who creates the lights of fire.

בָּרוּךְ אַתָּה יְיָ, אֱלֹהֵינוּ מֶלֶךְ הָעוֹלָם, הַמַּבְדִיל בֵּין קֹדֶשׁ לְחוֹל, בֵּין אוֹר לְחֹשֶׁךְ, בֵּין יִשְׂרָאֵל לָעַמִּים, בֵּין יוֹם הַשְּׁבִיעִי, לְשֵׁשֶׁת יְמֵי הַמַּעֲשֶׂה: בָּרוּךְ אַתָּה יְיָ, הַמַּבְדִיל בֵּין קֹדֶשׁ לְחוֹל:

BaruchAta Adonai, Eloheinu melech ha-olam, hamavdil bein kodesh l'chol, bein or l'choshech, bein Yisrael la-amim, bein yom hashvi-I l'sheishet y'mei ha-ma'aseh. Baruch Ata Adonai, hamavdil bein kodesh l'chol.

Blessed art Thou, Lord our God, King of the universe, who makes a distinction between sacred and secular, light and darkness, Israel and other peoples, the seventh day and the six days of labor. Blessed art Thou, Lord who makes a distinction between sacred and profane.

Hanukkah

Lighting Candles

בָּרוּךְ אַתָּה יְיָ אֱלֹהֵינוּ מֶלֶךְ הָעוֹלָם, אֲשֶׁר קִדְּשָׁנוּ בְּמִצְוֹתָיו וְצִוָּנוּ לְהַדְלִיק נֵר שֶׁל חֲנֻכָּה.

Baruch Ata Adonai, Eloheinu melech ha-olam, asher kidshanu b' mitzvotav v'tzivanu l'hadlik ner shel Hanukkah.

Blessed art Thou, Lord our God, King of the universe who has sanctified us with His commandments and ordained that we kindle the Hanukkah light.

בָּרוּךְ אַתָּה יְיָ אֱלֹהֵינוּ מֶלֶךְ הָעוֹלָם, שֶׁעָשָׂה נִסִּים לַאֲבוֹתֵינוּ בַּיָּמִים הָהֵם בַּזְּמַן הַזֶּה.

Baruch Ata Adonai, Eloheinu melech ha-olam, she'asa nisim lavotanu ba-y'mim hachem bazmon hazeh.

Blessed art Thou, Lord our God, King of the universe who has performed miracles for our forefathers in those days, at this time.

On the first night only

בָּרוּךְ אַתָּה יְיָ אֱלֹהֵינוּ מֶלֶךְ הָעוֹלָם, שֶׁהֶחֱיָנוּ וְקִיְּמָנוּ וְהִגִּיעָנוּ לַזְּמַן הַזֶּה.

Baruch Ata Adonai, Eloheinu melech ha-olam, shehecheyanu v'kiy'manu v'higi-anu lazman hazeh.

Blessed art Thou, Lord our God, King of the universe, who has granted us life and sustenance and permitted us to reach this time.

Ma-oz Tsur

מָעוֹז צוּר יְשׁוּעָתִי,   לְךָ נָאֶה לְשַׁבֵּחַ,
תִּכּוֹן בֵּית תְּפִלָּתִי,   וְשָׁם תּוֹדָה נְזַבֵּחַ,
לְעֵת תָּכִין מַטְבֵּחַ   מִצָּר הַמְנַבֵּחַ,
אָז אֶגְמֹר   בְּשִׁיר מִזְמוֹר   חֲנֻכַּת הַמִּזְבֵּחַ.

Ma-oz tsur ye-shu-a-ti, le-cha na-eh le-shabei-ach Ti-kon beit te-fi-la-ti, ve-sham toda ne-zabei-ach Le-eit ta-chin mat-bei-ach, mi-tsar ha-me-na-bei-ach, az eg-mor, be-shir miz-mor, cha-nu-kat ha-miz- bei-ach.

Rock of Ages

Rock of ages, let our song, praise Your saving power,
You, amid the raging foes, were our sheltering tower.
Furious, they assailed us, but your arm availed us,
And Your word, broke their sword, when our strength failed us.

Putting on a Tallis

בָּרוּךְ אַתָּה יְיָ אֱלֹהֵינוּ מֶלֶךְ הָעוֹלָם אֲשֶׁר קִדְּשָׁנוּ בְּמִצְוֹתָיו, וְצִוָּנוּ לְהִתְעַטֵּף בַּצִּיצִת.

Baruch Ata Adonai, Eloheinu melech ha-olam, asher kidshanu b' mitzvotav v'tzivanu, l'hit-atayf tzitzit.

Blessed art Thou, Lord our God, King of the universe who has sanctified us with His commandments and commanded us to enwrap ourself with tzitzit.

Affixing a Mezuzah

בָּרוּךְ אַתָּה יְיָ אֱלֹהֵינוּ מֶלֶךְ הָעוֹלָם, אֲשֶׁר קִדְּשָׁנוּ בְּמִצְוֹתָיו וְצִוָּנוּ לִקְבֹּעַ מְזוּזָה.

Baruch Ata Adonai, Eloheinu melech ha-olam, asher kidshanu b' mitzvotav v'tzivanu, likboa mezuzah.

Blessed art Thou, Lord our God, King of the universe who has sanctified us with His commandments and commanded us to affix a mezuzah.

Searching for Hametz

בָּרוּךְ אַתָּה יְיָ אֱלֹהֵינוּ מֶלֶךְ הָעוֹלָם, אֲשֶׁר קִדְּשָׁנוּ בְּמִצְוֹתָיו, עַל בְּעוּר חָמֵץ.

Baruch Ata Adonai, Eloheinu melech ha-olam, asher kidshanu b' mitzvotav v'tzivanu al be-ur ha-metz.

Blessed art Thou, Lord our God, King of the universe who has commanded us concerning the destruction of hametz.

Reading of the Torah

Before reading

בָּרוּךְ יְיָ הַמְבוֹרָךְ לְעוֹלָם וָעֶד:
בָּרוּךְ אַתָּה יְיָ אֱלֹהֵינוּ מֶלֶךְ הָעוֹלָם, אֲשֶׁר בָּחַר
בָּנוּ מִכָּל הָעַמִּים וְנָתַן לָנוּ אֶת תּוֹרָתוֹ: בָּרוּךְ
אַתָּה יְיָ, נוֹתֵן הַתּוֹרָה:

Barchu et Adonai ha-mevorach!
Baruch Adonai ha-mevorach le-olam va-ed!
Baruch ata Adonai, Elo-hanu melech ha-olam,
asher ba-char banu mi-kol ha-amim, ve-natan lanu
et Torah-to.
Baruch ata Adonai, no-tein ha-Torah.

Praise the Lord, to whom our praise is do!
Praised be the Lord, to whom our praise is do, now and forever!
Blessed is the Lord our God, Ruler of the universe, who has chosen us from all peoples by giving us His Torah. Blessed is the Lord, Giver of the Torah.

After Reading

בָּרוּךְ אַתָּה יְיָ אֱלֹהֵינוּ מֶלֶךְ הָעוֹלָם, אֲשֶׁר נָתַן
לָנוּ תּוֹרַת אֱמֶת, וְחַיֵּי עוֹלָם נָטַע בְּתוֹכֵנוּ:
בָּרוּךְ אַתָּה יְיָ, נוֹתֵן הַתּוֹרָה:

Baruch ata Adonai, Elohanu melech ha-olam,
asher natan lanu Torat emet, ve-cha-yei olam nata
beto-cheinu.
Baruch ata Adonai. no-tein ha-Torah.

Blessed is the Lord our God, Ruler of the universe,
who has given us a Torah of truth, implanting
within us eternal life. Blessed is the Lord, Giver of
the Torah

Death of a Loved One

Psalm 23
The Lord is my shepherd, I shall not want.
He makes me lie down in green pastures,
He leads beside still waters. He restores my soul.
He leads me in right paths for the sake of His
name.
Yae, though I walk through the valley of the
shadow of death, I shall fear no evil, for Thou art
with me; with rod and staff You comfort me. You
have set a table before me in the presence of my
enemies; You have annointed my head with oil,
my cup runneth over.
Surely mercy and goodness shallow follow me all
the days of my life and I shall dwell in the house of
the Lord forever.

Kaddish

יִתְגַּדַּל וְיִתְקַדַּשׁ שְׁמֵהּ רַבָּא. בְּעָלְמָא דִּי בְרָא
כִרְעוּתֵהּ, וְיַמְלִיךְ מַלְכוּתֵהּ בְּחַיֵּיכוֹן וּבְיוֹמֵיכוֹן וּבְחַיֵּי
דְכָל בֵּית יִשְׂרָאֵל. בַּעֲגָלָא וּבִזְמַן קָרִיב, וְאִמְרוּ אָמֵן:
יְהֵא שְׁמֵהּ רַבָּא מְבָרַךְ לְעָלַם וּלְעָלְמֵי עָלְמַיָּא:
יִתְבָּרַךְ וְיִשְׁתַּבַּח, וְיִתְפָּאַר וְיִתְרוֹמַם וְיִתְנַשֵּׂא וְיִתְהַדָּר
וְיִתְעַלֶּה וְיִתְהַלָּל שְׁמֵהּ דְּקֻדְשָׁא בְּרִיךְ הוּא לְעֵלָּא מִן
כָּל בִּרְכָתָא וְשִׁירָתָא, תֻּשְׁבְּחָתָא וְנֶחֱמָתָא, דַּאֲמִירָן
בְּעָלְמָא, וְאִמְרוּ אָמֵן:
יְהֵא שְׁלָמָא רַבָּא מִן שְׁמַיָּא וְחַיִּים טוֹבִים עָלֵינוּ וְעַל
כָּל יִשְׂרָאֵל, וְאִמְרוּ אָמֵן:
עֹשֶׂה שָׁלוֹם בִּמְרוֹמָיו הוּא בְּרַחֲמָיו יַעֲשֶׂה שָׁלוֹם
עָלֵינוּ וְעַל כָּל יִשְׂרָאֵל, וְאִמְרוּ אָמֵן:

*Yitgadal v'yitkadash sh'mei raba. B'alma di v'ra
chirutei,v'yamlich malchutei b'cha-yeichon
uv-yomeichon, uv-cha-yei d'chol bet Yisrael,
ba'agala u-vizman kariv, v'imru Amein.
Y'hei sh'mei raba m'vorach l'alam ul-almei
almaya.
Yitbarach v'yishtabach v'yitpa'ar v'yitromam
v'yitnasei, v'yithadad v'yitaleh v'yit halal sh'mei
d'kudsha b'rich Hu. L'eilah min kol birchata
v'shirashta, tushb'chata v'nechemata, da'amiran
b'alma v'imru Amein.
Y'hei sh'lama raba min sh'maya, v'chayim aleinu
v'al kol Yisrael, v'imru Amein.
Oseh shalom bim'romav, hu ya'aseh shlalom
aleinnu v'al kol Yisrael, v/imru Amein.*

Exalted and hollowed be God's great name In this world of his creation
May His will be fulfilled and His soveignty revealed in the days of your lifetime and the life of the whole house of Israel speedily and soon, and say, Amen.

Be His great name blessed forever, Yea to all eternity.

Be the name of the most Holy One blessed, praised and honored, extolled and glorified, adored and exhalted supremely. Blessed be He, beyond all blessings and hymns, praises and consolations that may be uttered in this world. And say, Amen.

May peace abundant descend from heaven with life for us and Israel, and say, Amen.

May He who creates the harmony of the spheres create peace for us and all Israel, and say, Amen.

JEWISH
RESOURCES
AND
HELPFUL
NUMBERS

NATIONAL JEWISH ORGANIZATIONS

Chabad
www.chabad.org

Orthodox Union
www.ou.org

United Synagogue of Conservative Judaism
www.uscj.org

Union of American Hebrew Congregations
www.uahc.org

American Jewish Congress
(212) 879-4500
www.ajc.org

American Israeli Public Affairs Committee
(AIPAC)
(202) 639-5200
www.aipac.org

Hillel
(202) 857-6560
www.hillel.org

United Jewish Communities (formerly UJA)
(212) 284-6500
www.ujc.org

Jewish National Fund
www.jnf.org

ANTI-DEFAMATION LEAGUE
OF B'NAI B'RITH
www.adl.org

Albuquerque	(505) 843-7177
Arizona	(602) 274-0991
Atlanta	(404) 262-3470
Boston	(617) 330-9696
Chicago	(312) 782-5080
Cleveland	(216) 579-9600
Columbus	(614) 621-0601
Connecticut	(203) 787-4281
Dallas	(214) 960-0342
D.C.	(202) 452-8310
Denver	(303) 321-7177
Detroit	(313) 355-3730
Houston	(713) 627-3490
Los Angeles	(310) 446-8000
Miami	(305) 373-6306
Minneapolis	(612) 338-7816
New Jersey	(201) 669-9700
New Orleans	(504) 522-9534
NY City	(212) 490-2525
NY State	(518) 271-6011
Omaha	(402) 333-1303
Orange County	(714) 973-4733
Palm Beach County	(407) 832-7144
Philadelphia	(412) 471-1050
San Diego	(619) 293-3770
San Francisco	(415) 981-3500
Seattle	(206) 448-5349
St. Louis	(314) 432-6868
Virginia	(804) 455-9002

JEWISH FRATERNITIES AND SORORITIES
Fraternities
>Alpha Epsilon Pi - *www.aepi.org*
>Sigma Alpha Mu - *www.sam.org*
>Zeta Beta Tau - *www.zbt.org*

Sororities
>Alpha Epsilon Phi - *www.aephi.org*
>Delta Phi Epsilon - *www.dphie.org*
>Sigma Delta Tau -*www.sigmadeltatau.com*

JEWISH WEB RESOURCES
>*www.virtualjerusalem.com*
>*www.mavensearch.com*
>*www.shamash.com*
>*www.kotelkam.com*

NATIONAL HEALTH ORGANIZATIONS
Alcoholics Anonymous
>(212) 870-9400
>*www.aa.org*

Narcotics Anonymous
>*www.na.org*

Center for Disease Control
>STD Hotline   1-800-227-8922
>HIV Hotline 1-800-342-2437
>*www.cdc.gov*

Overeaters Anonymous
>See Local Phone Book
>*www.overeatersanonymous.org*

CALENDAR OF JEWISH HOLIDAYS
All holidays begin at sundown the night before

	2001	2002	2003	2004	2005	2006
Tu B'Shevat	Feb. 8	Jan. 28	Jan. 18	Feb. 7	Jan. 25	Feb. 13
Purim	March 9	Feb. 26	March 18	March 7	March 25	March 14
Passover	April 8	March 28	April 17	April 6	April 24	April 13
Yom Hashoah	April 19	April 9	April 29	April 18	May 5	April 25
Yom Hazikaron	April 25	April 16	May 6	April 25	May 11	May 2
Yom Ha'Atzmaut	April 26	April 17	May 7	April 26	May 12	May 3
Shavuot	May 28	May 17	June 6	May 26	June 13	June 2
Rosh Hashanah	Sept. 18	Sept. 7	Sept. 27	Sept. 16	Oct. 4	Sept. 23
Yom Kippur	Sept. 27	Sept. 16	Oct. 6	Sept. 25	Oct. 13	Oct. 2
Sukkot	Oct. 2	Sept. 21	Oct. 11	Sept. 30	Oct. 18	Oct. 7
Simchat Torah	Oct. 10	Sept. 29	Oct. 19	Oct. 8	Oct. 26	Oct. 15
Hanukkah	Dec. 10	Nov. 30	Dec. 20	Dec. 8	Dec. 26	Dec. 16

BIBLIOGRAPHY

Fitzhenry, Robert I, ed. The Harper Book Of Quatations, New York : Harper Collins, 1993.

Grottesman, Greg. College Survival, New York : Macmillan, 1994.

Kertzer, Morris N. What is a Jew, New York : Macmillan, 1978.

Levine, Samuel. You Take Jesus, I'll Take God. Los Angeles : Hamoroh Press, 1980.

Parrot, Andrea ed. Acquaintence Rape, The Hidden Crime, Wiley : New York, 1991.

Wanderer, Zev. and Tracy Cabot. Letting Go, New York : Dell, 1987.

TO ORDER COPIES OF:

YOU TAKE JESUS, I'LL TAKE GOD BY SAMUEL LEVINE

SEND $6.95 TO:
    HAMOROH PRESS
    P.O. BOX 48862
    LOS ANGELES, CA 90048